HEAR THE
PENNIES DROPPING

by
Gwyneth J. Whilsmith

First printing August 1987
Setting and design by
Gunbyfield Publishing Limited
Box 37
10A The Square
Goderich, Ontario, Canada
N7A 3Y5

Canadian Cataloguing in Publication Data

    Whilsmith, Gwyneth J.
    Hear the pennies dropping

    ISBN 0-921078-00-5

    1. Whilsmith, Gwyneth J.   2. Saskatchewan — Economic
    conditions — 1905-1945.*   3. Saskatchewan — History —
    1905-1945.*   4. Depressions — 1929 — Canada.
    I. Title.

    FC3523.1.W45A3 1987   971.24'02'0924   C87-094807-5
    PR9199.3.W45A3 1987

HEAR THE PENNIES DROPPING

Dedicated

To my family ...
Those who went before,
Those who still walk with me,
And all those who follow.

CONTENTS

~

CHAPTER ONE

Age of Innocence

I was a child of the Great Depression. When it struck in 1929, I was six years old and living with my parents, my older sister Lola, and two brothers, Carfrey and Arthur, on a farm in Saskatchewan. Ten years later, when it ended, I had just moved with them to Ontario. Although I was very young, no ten years of my life affected me more.

It wasn't until I was nearing adulthood that I realized the Depression was caused by the collapse of the economic systems of the world. I may have heard vaguely about the *Crash of '29*, but to me, a child growing up in Saskatchewan, the Depression simply meant years of drought, hail, grasshoppers, rolling black dust clouds, failed crops, and the struggle of my parents to keep life more or less normal through a desperate period of time.

I do not write this story because my family was in any way different or more notable than any other. In fact, just the opposite is true: my parents were the same as thousands of other ordinary people who lived through that period of hard times with a kind of desperate faith and a courage laced with laughter as well as tears. They had to count their pennies, and know where each one fell. Squandering and waste were deemed sinful, and in every area of their lives they learned to "make do" with what they had.

In many ways, it was also an age of innocence ... an age that has all but disappeared. Despite the difficulties and tragedy caused by Nature and, sometimes, the suffering caused by the hardness of others, it was a time when almost everyone believed in God, that right would prevail and that justice would be done. There was the belief that if you worked hard enough and long enough, you would finally be rewarded.

1

There was sex, liquor, and even drugs, but they didn't permeate lives as they do now. For better or worse marriages lasted, and I must have been into my teens before I even met a divorced person. Families stuck together, were not fragmented, and we children were secure in our homes with one mother and one father. Our world might have been hard at times, but every day we could count on the things that mattered most remaining the same. There was stability in our lives, despite the Depression, and a confidence that with God's help everything would work out all right.

Much of the naiveté faded, however, when a bloody war — and not new and better social policies of government — brought the hard times to an end. Later, when victory was finally won, and after many of our friends and relatives had been killed or maimed, we learned that war was, at least in part, manipulated by warmongers who amassed great fortunes through the sale of arms ... and we lost more of our innocence.

Since then, we've watched our children move into a world of hard drugs, pornography, violence, pollution, exploitative sex, family breakups, and the threat of nuclear war, all of which affect even the youngest of our grandchildren and which are, in my opinion, far more destructive than the Great Depression ever was. It's not surprising that innocence and optimism seem to be disappearing, and that there are many pessimistic skeptics around.

However, for the most part, whenever I speak to other people who lived through the Depression, I continue to find optimism and faith showing through. Perhaps it's just one of the marks that's on us, and a legacy we should try to pass on.

~

CHAPTER TWO

A Promise to Keep

I t's difficult to say what is my earliest memory. I know I listened so intently to stories of my babyhood that I thought I remembered certain incidents when, in actuality, I probably didn't. However, one event that happened when I was three or four stands out with clarity — my christening. I have no idea why I wasn't christened as an infant, but in any event the deed took place in the

dining room of our farm house with a tall, sombre minister standing between Bubbles (my friend, who was six weeks younger than I) and me, and pouring water over our heads. It dribbled down on my brown velvet dress and, to my horror, a few drops hit my brand new Buster Brown shoes which buttoned at the ankles. Our parents stood facing us, and I can still see my mother's lovely face framed in soft, dark hair, smiling encouragement so I wouldn't be too upset.

Memory is such a funny thing. Sometimes you just get snatches of recall, while other events can be played back like an old movie. Then there are great stretches that are completely blocked out so that you wonder where in the world you were and what you were doing at the time. I do remember one day,

Mother with me, taken at the back of our house about the time of my christening.

however, when I made a promise to Dad. I was about five, and having hopped up beside him on the board plank that served as a seat on the top of his grain wagon box, we set out to deliver a load of wheat to the elevator in

3

Dad's oat crop of 1923.

Brock, our small Saskatchewan town. I loved being with Dad and tagged along with him whenever I could; he always made me feel so loved and important. "Yes," he would drawl, "1923 was a good year. We harvested our best crop of oats, bought our first car (and then with a twinkle he would add), and you were born!" How I'd squirm with delight!

I joined the family rather late, my sister Lola being ten, and my brothers Carfrey and Arthur eight and six. Later, I was told Mother wasn't exactly overjoyed at having another child, until Dad convinced her it would be wonderful to have a baby in the house again. Lola, however, wasn't as easily swayed. When it was announced that a new baby girl had arrived, she retorted tartly, "Well, I'd sooner have had a winter coat!" Nevertheless, she assured me that as soon as she laid eyes on me her heart melted, and from that day to this she has been my true and constant champion. I have no doubt that, next to Mother and Dad, she has been the person who influenced me most.

Since she and my brothers were off at school by the time I made my appearance, a good deal of my young life was spent alone, or following Dad around as he worked in the barn and farm yard.

That particular day, as we drove the five lazy miles to town, I was purely content. It was a gentle fall day. The dry, gray prairie grass waved softly as our team of bay Clydesdales plodded along steadily, the dust from the narrow road swirling in tiny clouds around their white leg feathers. The wide blue prairie sky arched sublimely above us, while the sun, travelling south and losing its scorching midsummer heat, just warmed our backs comfortably. It was a time of peace, a time for dreaming.

Sharing dreams with Dad was easy. A quiet-toned man who spoke only when he had something to say, he was a wonderful listener, one with whom I could blather freely and even share some of the adventures I took with my imaginary friends.

Because there were no children close by to play with, I spent hours with make-believe companions who were as real to me as live friends, and who played an important role in my life. I was the Princess Jean who was kind and good, but interestingly, I had a twin sister who was not good and who played all kinds of nasty tricks on people. We lived with other make-believe companions in the parched back yard where Dad had put in a good-sized sandbox (my castle), a swing held up by two telephone poles (my throne), and a revolving teeter totter (my chariot).

4

Of course one child cannot have much fun on a teeter totter, so Dad tied a bag of sand (about my weight) to one end, with whom I spent hours riding along in my chariot. I say "whom" because this was no bag of sand, but a faithful companion, Boo-boo, who shared all my secrets and adventures.

A karagana hedge skirted the yard, and down its thick, spiny rows the three of us, Boo-boo, the bad princess, and I, crept on secret missions, or sometimes charged into noisy, daring escapades with other imaginary comrades. These created friends came from far distant lands, speaking strange languages in which I was always conversant. You might say I was speaking in tongues long before I ever heard of Pentecostalism!

Carf and Art loved nothing better than to sneak up and listen to my animated conversations, breaking them up with derogatory snickering and teasing me for "talking to myself" until I cried and stamped my feet. But despite their constant heckling, nothing could prevent me from living this extraordinary, imaginary life.

In sub-zero weather, bundled up in long underwear, thick woolen stockings, and a heavy long coat, I'd stagger up the steep banks of crusted snow that blazed like diamonds in the bright sun and piled up around the hedge. Of course I had never heard of Mount Everest, yet I commanded many a hazardous climbing expedition over those deep drifts with an enthusiasm that might have surprised Sir Edmund Hillary.

This was long before television, and looking back I wonder from where in the depths of my mind I conjured up all those fantasies and people in such detail that I knew exactly how they looked and what they wore. Perhaps it is true, as Jung suggests, that we know more than we know, that deep down in our unconscious there is accumulated knowledge from ages and ancestors long gone. Perhaps, too, as children we are open to this inner knowledge and better able to assimilate it than when we are grown too wise.

Anyway, as I rode along with my father, dreaming about this life I led, I remarked confidently, "Some day I'm going to write a book about my life." He squinted off to the distant rim of the prairies, a gentle smile playing on his lips. "I hope I'll be the first to read it." I assured him that he would.

As I grew older, I began to think my life anything but interesting, and chafed with envy when others travelled to faraway places or had fascinating or worthwhile jobs. It's only recently that I've come to realize that every life has its interesting points, that everyone has something to share.

However, Dad will not read this account. I left it too late. He died in 1976 at the age of 86, and Lola, Carf, Art, and I adored him to the end. Nevertheless, I'm sure he'd be pleased that I finally got around to keeping the first half of the promise, anyway.

CHAPTER THREE

You Can't Go Back

I n 1978, a far-flung clarion summoned back all the students who had attended the Brock Brick School between the year 1912, when it was opened, and 1958, when it was torn down to make room for building lots. Hundreds of former pupils answered the call and streamed back from as far away as New Zealand, swelling the tiny Saskatchewan hamlet until its seams were bursting.

Lola and I flew out from Toronto to Saskatoon and caught a bus across the prairie to Brock, where we hadn't visited for years. It was a perfect western day, bright blue sky, clear dry air, and wide horizons. The miles and minutes flew by as the bus swept us past scenes almost forgotten. We were anxious to see the farm on which we had been raised, but because we didn't recognize it quickly enough we passed by with only a glimpse. It was like travelling in a dream: things looked vaguely familiar, but not quite right.

And that's how it seemed the whole reunion weekend. Most of us arrived the evening before the official festivities began, so by twilight the streets were overflowing with people strolling from house to house, meeting old friends, and viewing landmarks not seen for decades. But the houses were not quite as large, nor the streets as wide, nor the buildings as many, nor the people as young as we remembered. Still, confabulation and laughter rang in the night and the lights burned late as the "catching up" went on till dawn.

Next morning it was raining, and those of us who hadn't been back West for awhile felt that this, too, was planned for our benefit. We'd almost forgotten the thick, sticky gumbo that builds up on your feet — until we had to pick our way through it to register at the new school.

With our name tags securely attached, we turned to search the sea of faces for someone who looked even a little bit familiar. Thank goodness for name tags, but still I was sometimes mystified. When a good-looking, gray-haired man pumped my hand enthusiastically and exclaimed, "How are ya, Gwyn? Great to see ya," I couldn't place his face or name. Happily, someone else caught his eye so he moved off to extend another hearty greeting.

It was impossible to keep anyone's attention long enough for conversation because all eyes roved constantly over the crowd, not wanting to miss anyone. Old acquaintances with whom I was most anxious to meet were engrossed with other people or dashing about trying to see everyone at once.

Finally, I detached myself from the mêlée and backed off to a corner from where I viewed the back-slapping, the hugging, and the delighted squeals of recognition. It was strange, I thought, that the people who seemed to remember me best were younger than I, until I realized that I too was recalling with more clarity the students who were a bit older than I. The older students had left a more lasting impression than some of our contemporaries.

In any event, Lola and I were happily lodged with our good friends, Zella and Gordon Ham, and like everyone else were wined, dined, and entertained for three packed-full days. Our throats got raw and our voices failed as our heads rang from too much talking and not enough sleep. The local citizens, who threw open their homes, also threw open their hearts, and must have been reeling with fatigue as they thankfully waved the last of us down the road. I've always hoped they felt it was worth all their efforts.

And what was it worth to us who returned? I'm sure most of us experienced high tides as well as low ones. As for me, who had been away for a long time, it brought me back to my roots and made me more perceptive of the debt I owed. I sat in the small white frame church that my grandfather, Abram, had helped build. I looked over the land that had held out false promises and cheated my dad, despite all his labour during the Depression. My eyes filled with tears over the house he and Mother had built with high hopes, and where they had raised the four of us with such love and sacrifice.

At the turn of the century, there were only miles of bald prairie covered with grass. Now there is productive farm land dotted with oil wells and tilled and harvested by immense and expensive equipment about which our pioneer ancestors could not have even dreamed.

More enthusiasm, gutsy determination, heartache, and hard work went into opening up that small Saskatchewan community than most of us can imagine. As children, we had no realization that our parents were the pioneers, the heroes and heroines who broke the land, erected the first schools, planned the first churches, and threw up the first telephone lines. How could we know what a debt we owed them?

I learned something else by going back. I learned that life has a way of evening up the score. During the Depression, there was a family of eight children poorer than most of us. Those who lived on farms at least had enough to eat, but this family, living in a shabby, tiny house on the outskirts of town, was sometimes destitute. The parents were a genteel English couple who were ill-fitted to make their way through those cruel times. The father was a printer and an artist, and Mother bought some of his paintings for a few precious dollars, even though her own supply of money was less than ample. When the garden produced, she shared it with them, and sometimes Dad left a hundred-pound bag of flour at their door when he cashed in his wheat. Mother took great interest in the younger children and often brought them to our house for holidays so she could fatten them up with her country cooking.

Most of that family was back to the school reunion, all looking very affluent. One brother, a genius, had invented a device that made him a millionaire. This was the poor, skinny kid who played with me in the back-yard sandbox, yet fifty-five years later, he looked so worldly and successful with his beautiful, sophisticated wife I was too shy to go up and speak to him for fear that he might not remember me!

There was at least one other millionaire among us, and I suspect there were more. Some, who had struggled to put themselves through university, had flourishing careers in the professions and in several types of businesses. The biggest surprise, however, was the wild, reckless teenager who had run away from home to ride the rails. He came back as an evangelist and preached the sermon at the interdenominational service. By contrast, the boy who was the brightest and most popular in my class, who had shown great potential, whose family had more money than the rest of us, was tragically fighting a losing battle against alcoholism.

And then there was Joe. Joe was a thin little waif from a large Ukrainian family who had arrived at school unable to speak English. A sad bit of a thing with his brown wiry hair sticking straight in the air, he often had nothing more than a few slices of bread in his lunch pail. But one day after opening his pail he began to holler and laugh with uncontrollable joy as he held aloft, for all to see, the unexpected, marvellous treat of a small brown sausage. His delight at such a small luxury was something I carried around with me for most of my life, haunted by the feeling that maybe I should have been more helpful to that little boy. It was natural, then, that one of the first people I asked for when I went back for the reunion was Joe. "Joe?" answered my friends. "Joe's done OK. He married the schoolteacher and is one of the most successful farmers in the district!"

8

Thank goodness. At last, Joe was off my back.

So, what does one learn from going back to a school reunion? Many things, not the least of which is that life doesn't necessarily end up the way it started. Returning also stirred up a cloud of memories that swirled and danced around me, demanding my attention for months. As I groped my way through them I experienced some solace, some regret, and some pain. Even during the hullaballoo of the reunion I had a sense of loneliness, of something missing, of expectations unfulfilled. It took me a long time to understand why.

In the first place, instead of finding the friends of my childhood, I found strangers with whom I had nothing in common. Many of our old neighbours, my parents' friends, were gone, and in some cases even their houses were missing, having been demolished to make way for larger wheat fields or more modern buildings.

But I knew that something else was causing my irrational feelings of grief. When I moved from the West to Ontario to go to school, I was only 15. It was a traumatic experience to leave behind everyone and everything I had ever known ... a terrible loss. To the community, however, I was just one young girl leaving, a slight loss, perhaps, but nothing compared to the deprivation I felt.

Each time I went back I was filled with anticipation and excitement, only to leave, again, with a sadness hanging over me. Not that I wasn't made welcome or greeted warmly, because I certainly was, but to all those people I was just one person coming to visit, while I was trying to return to everything and everyone who had played so important a role in my young years.

Finally, I realized I was grieving for the way things used to be, but hadn't been for decades and, of course, would never be again. As I sat alone in Zella's car, parked at the foot of the laneway of my parents' old home, and looked at the lilac bushes Mother had planted more than fifty years before, awash with purple and white blossoms, a dam burst within me. But I was healed of a sorrow I had harboured for many years.

"You can never go back." We hear that said many times, and it's true. Nothing remains static, neither people nor places. We return, and because everything looks so alien we feel lonely and unsettled.

But it does force us to see the reality of ourselves, because we too have changed more than we sometimes care to admit. We have moved away, and not always just in physical miles. So, although you can take the trip, it's true you can never go back.

Still, after all the memories were sifted through, there was the essence of how things were and what I was and still am.

~

9

CHAPTER FOUR

At seventeen.

My Mother, Charlotte

harlotte (Lottie) Maria Hammond (for some reason Mother always hated the name Maria and wouldn't own it) was born near Grand Valley, Ontario, in 1892, the youngest of eleven children, seven girls and four boys. Born with a veil over her face, which indicated a life of good fortune in those days, she was a beautiful child, adored and pampered by her large family.

Her father, William, died when he was only fifty-six, but her mother, Jane Westover, lived to be eighty and was known far and wide for her acts of charity in the community. A self-taught nurse and midwife, she was often awakened in the night by a knock at the door or a call at her window to hurry off, sometimes by horse and buggy, sometimes by walking several miles, to the house where she was needed. She took great interest in the babies she delivered, and was respected and loved by everyone who knew her.

Mother's family, while a large one, was also a happy one, with much friendly bantering and laughter around the table that stretched the length of the kitchen. The older married members all lived close by, so they came home often for family gatherings. Mother remembered Christmas as a time of delight, with everyone there to

William and Jane Hammond on their wedding day, 1870.

join in the fun. The younger children's stockings were hung on the railing of an open staircase so Santa could put in an orange, nuts, and candy. One Christmas, little Lottie was thrilled to find a tiny gold ring in the toe of her stocking, something to be cherished forever.

Her eldest sister, Mary, was at least twenty years older, and had been half-adopted by a sister of Grandmother Hammond who had married a wealthy man. His name was William Warnock, and the story goes that he went to the California Gold Rush and made a strike. However, when coming out on horseback with $20,000 worth of gold, he was robbed of everything, even his clothes and horse. Undaunted, he went back to the gold fields, working for another miner until he made enough money to stake out another claim. This time, he apparently struck it rich. Fortunately, banks had opened up in California by that time so he could deposit his gold and get a credit note rather than bring out his wealth on his person and risk being robbed again.

He came back to Canada, married my grandmother's sister Mary, and built and furnished a beautiful house in Fergus. Because they had married late in life and had no children, they took special interest in Mother's sister, Mary, who had been named after her aunt. They saw that she received a good education, and in fact, sent her to Alma College in St. Thomas in its very early days. When the old aunt died in the 1890s, Aunt Mary inherited the furnishings of the house. She built an addition to my grandmother's farm home and brought in the red plush carpets and all the beautiful hand-carved furniture which Mother used to describe to us in detail. Happily, one of the chairs now graces my own livingroom.

When I was small, I never tired of Mother talking about what seemed to be her enchanted childhood. While she ironed on the kitchen table, I played underneath with my kittens and listened, enraptured. "It was almost like living in fairyland," she'd say, "with six fairy godmothers (her older sisters) who supplied all my desires — dolls of every shape and size, beautiful frocks and pinafores, and velvet bonnets with matching coats."

She bewitched me with stories about her playhouse "just inside the picket fence, under the pear tree, beside the pump," and about riding her old horse, Nell, and going fishing in the stream with a bent pin, and how proud she was to bring home a small pail of fish. She recounted "sugaring off" in the spring, and going berry picking, and the delicious red raspberry wine her mother made up for a drink. Her word pictures were so beautiful that it's not much wonder that to me, a child living on the dry prairies, they were, indeed, like fairytales.

When Lottie left school she went to Grand Valley to train as a milliner and to concoct those wonderful hats piled with flowers, ribbons, and veils that were worn during the early part of this century. She had learned to sew from her mother, a talented seamstress, and all her days Mother turned out beautiful things.

Mother and Dad's courtship lasted four years, from the time she was sixteen and he seventeen. Two years before, however, when she had first seen him, a shy, brown-eyed youth, she had known without a doubt, "He's the boy I'm going to marry." They always recalled those courtship years as being wonderfully carefree and blissfully happy. There were picnics for two by the stream in the bush where they picked wild raspberries, and long romantic rides home from church socials on the high buggy seat with Dad letting the reins go slack to allow the horse to meander along the narrow road while Mother snuggled on his shoulder. They remained romantics all their lives, their eyes always misting over the old songs like "When You and I Were Young, Maggie," and "When Your Hair Has Turned to Silver."

They were married in their tiny country church (Monticello) with Mother's sister Mabel and her husband Tommy Colbeck at their sides. Dad would often recall, years later, how Mother tittered and chirped all through the ceremony, seemingly quite oblivious to the solemnity of the day!

Some of the days that followed were not quite as happy. Soon after they were married, and against Mother's judgement, they were persuaded by Dad's parents to join them in farming in Saskatchewan.

Dad rode in a boxcar loaded with his horses and cows, furniture and other household goods, while Mother followed in a passenger car. In those days, the rich travelled comfortably, taking their meals in an opulent dining car with white linen tablecloths, gleaming silver, and fine china. But if you were an ordinary person you took your food and cooked it on a stove at the end of the car. And you slept on blankets spread over the slatted wooden seats. After three or four days you were stiff, grubby, and bone-tired.

The end of the arduous trip didn't bring as much joy to Mother as it should have, however. "When I got off the train and looked around," she wrote in her diary, I thought, 'Well, this surely must be next door to hell!'"

If she found the flat, barren landscape of Saskatchewan depressing, she found the living arrangements almost unbearable, sharing a three-room, tarpaper shack with Dad's parents. After the easy-going jollity of her mother's home, she found her father-in-law's attitudes harsh and unbending. Worse still, because space was scarce, all her wedding gifts and belongings were stored in another shack where the mice destroyed everything, even the felts of her organ, a gift from her mother.

When Dad's parents moved into town, Mother tried to make the little gray shack more liveable. It was a shell of a place through which the icy winds

The little gray prairie shack, Mother and Dad's first home in Saskatchewan. From left, Mother, Grandfather Cann, Uncle Art, and Dad, who is holding the horses.

whistled, and she pasted cotton sugar sacks on the walls in a valiant attempt to make it warmer. They finally bought another farm and built a snug house on it, and although things were much better, she still missed her old home and the rolling green hills of Ontario.

During the Depression, anxiety frayed her nerves and lined her beautiful face. She was often sharp-tongued and angry, not at us so much as at the whole world and how it was then. A nervous twitch appeared at the corner of her soft wide mouth, and her hair went prematurely gray.

Perhaps her own unhappiness made her more sensitive to the needs of others. Her heart was as big and soft as a feather pillow, and throughout her life she was always ready to assist those who were down and out. Because our house was only a quarter of a mile from the main road, we received at our door more than our share of hobos looking for food. They were never turned away. At the kitchen table, Mother listened to their lonely stories, wept with them, and sent them away encouraged and full. It angered and broke her mother's heart to see those desperate young men riding the rails or hitch-hiking across the country, sleeping in the open and living off handouts. She knew that, but for the grace of God, there went her own two sons.

While to such as these her generosity knew no bounds, she had another side. If she perceived someone to be lazy or unworthy of assistance, nothing could budge her to open her heart or purse strings. She had a tiger-fierce loyalty to her family and friends, but if someone got in her bad books she

13

could be an unrelenting and sometimes unforgiving adversary.

One thing she could never do was bid a graceful farewell to someone she loved. I vividly remember the day Art left for Normal School in Saskatoon, leaving home for the first time and looking so young and vulnerable. Dad loaded the suitcases in the car and was ready to drive off to the railway station when, suddenly, Mother was gone. And although we all looked around anxiously, she was nowhere to be found. To avoid the pain of saying good-bye, she hid in the barn and remained there long after Art was on his way, until she was in control of the grief she felt at having one of her young fly the nest. I knew well enough to leave her alone for the rest of the day.

She was not always sad, however, and on good days she pealed forth the merriest, most infectious laughter I have ever heard. A born prankster who loved nothing better than tricking some unsuspecting soul, she looked forward to April Fool's Day with child-like delight. No one was safe from her that day, especially not our father. She'd fill the sugarbowl with salt so that after he took his first big mouthful of porridge he'd run choking and coughing to the back door to spit it out. Mother would sway over the stove, eyes crinkled shut, spluttering with uncontrollable mirth.

One Hallowe'en, she made up a mask of flour and water and pressed it over her face, which gave her a ghoulish appearance far more ghastly than Frankenstein's monster. Wrapped in a sheet, she crouched in the karagana hedge and jumped out at me and May Clifford, a friend of hers, while we were making our way through the pitch dark from the backhouse. Scared witless, we flew screaming to the kitchen door while the apparition chased close behind until it collapsed on the ground, overcome with laughter. Somehow, May and I didn't find it quite so funny.

May Clifford was an Irish girl who had come to Canada in the early '20s to marry her sweetheart, only to find on her arrival that he had changed his mind. Devastated, with no one to turn to, she was taken in by Mother until her broken heart mended. She eventually settled in Saskatoon and got a job as a librarian.

I think Mother loved May for her marvellous wit. When she came to visit, our house rang with their laughter. Tears streaming down their faces, they held their aching sides while they wobbled around, sometimes even wetting their underwear, which only made them laugh harder!

May's visits were anticipated by me, too. She seemed so glamorous in her pretty clothes, bright silk

Mother's good Irish friend, May Clifford.

14

scarves, and lovely perfume. Another thing that excited me was that she brought boxes of discarded library books. It was like getting boxes of gold!

The most bizarre things struck Mother and May as funny. The sound of Dad retching with the stomach flu made Mother stuff her apron in her mouth to hold back gales of laughter while May ran outside to hide hers. A persistent fly landing on the bald head of the exasperated minister had them shaking the whole long church pew. (Many, many years later when May visited us in Ontario, she and Mother were just the same, still laughing until their sides almost burst, and still wetting their underwear!)

Some of Mother's family could be very testy, including Mother herself. Occasionally a couple of them would get into a scrap so serious it would stop them from speaking to each other. However, they could never endure the silence for any length of time and would soon be back laughing together, forgetting completely what the spat had been about.

All of her brothers and sisters had great senses of humour and laughed at themselves as readily as they laughed at others. Uncle George, Mother's oldest brother, was certainly no exception. An imp of a man with bright twinkling eyes, he may have played one last prank even after he died.

Mother and five of her sisters, all of whom lived to be over eighty. From the left, Till, who died when she was more than a hundred years old, Rachel, Mary, Mabel, Alice, and Lottie (Mother). Another sister, Belle, died in her thirties.

When Mother and two of her sisters arrived at his funeral they were informed by the funeral director that there were two funerals that day, and he directed them to the room where Uncle George lay. But when the three sombre sisters approached the casket, they found a stranger lying in it.

"That's not George!" whispered my startled mother.

"No, that's not George," agreed Aunt Mabel as she bent over the corpse.

"It *could* be George," Aunt Alice murmured, peering even more closely.

"No, no, that's *definitely* not George," insisted Mother as she and Aunt Mabel wheeled Aunt Alice out of that room and marched her into the next.

Again they approached the casket.

"Is *that* George?" asked Mother incredulously.

"It *might* be George," said Aunt Mabel dubiously.

"*That's* not George," pronounced Aunt Alice emphatically.

There was a stir behind them, and turning, they saw several weeping strangers entering the room.

"You're right, that's *not* George!"

With sheepish, downcast eyes, they slid silently through the startled mourners and out into the hall.

Of course the first corpse was their brother George, but because he was in such an unlively state they had failed to recognize him. That was enough to send those three dizzy sisters into hysterics. With hats pulled down over their eyes and their handkerchiefs pressed to their mouths, they chortled and shuddered all through the service, pretending to be overcome with grief. And as their shoulders shook uncontrollably, their poor, embarrassed husbands tried to pretend they didn't know them.

Leaving the funeral home, still gurgling and groaning, they collapsed in the car, wiping up their tears and letting their laughter finally burst forth. "Oh, my," gasped Mother, "Wouldn't George *die* if he could see us?"

Mother left us with more than a sense of humour and compassion, however. She instructed us well in the subject of beauty, and with a thankful heart I wrote this poem about her shortly after she died in her eighty-first year.

She Taught Us Beauty _____

Sometimes when I'm at the mirror
fixing my hair
or smoothing my lipstick,
I see
my mother's hands ...
> *the same shape*
> *the same nails*
> *the same gestures.*
I take my hands
and study them wondering
if they'll leave a heritage
of beauty as hers did.

Her hands were never still
and left a treasure-house
of fine stitched quilts,
yards of snowy lace in intricate patterns
fashioned with a crochet hook;
dolls exquisitely dressed in every race,

oil paintings of the flowers she loved
and many other precious things.
Though often ill
she never knew the sin of boredom
and just before she died at 81
she talked of taking up
ceramics.

She was not schooled
but could discern the work
of a master artist
with the best of critics ...
It was as though she had
an inner eye
for all things lovely.
"Look up and see the rainbow"
she would command us
puddling in the mud.
Sometimes she'd prod us out of bed
to make us fill our eyes and minds
with the sunrise melting up
in golden rivulets upon a dark gray sky.
A bird's song, sparkling water,
a dead tree outlined on winter sunsets,
all this she taught to us
as Beauty.

One night I remember
when very young
we two stood breathless,
close together in the frigid air
watching the northern lights
move and play across a velvet prairie sky
in such unspeakable glory
we could only hold each other's hand
in silent awful wonderment
and cry.
Thank God for Mother's hands
and for a life
that added Beauty
to my own. _____

~

17

CHAPTER FIVE

My Father, Alex

I f Mother was volatile and sometimes unpredictable, our stocky, handsome dad was the embodiment of steadfastness and calm. The bulwark of my youthful world, I knew that everything was safe and sound as long as he was there.

His grandfather, George, emigrated from England to Wellington County in Ontario in the 1840s. He married a pretty French girl, Mary Anne Deloane, and began to raise a large family. George was an itinerate Methodist preacher-farmer, apparently more preacher than farmer as he was often away on his rounds, leaving Mary Anne and the ten children with the heavy farm work, which included clearing the bush off the land.

One of his sons was Abram, Dad's father, and he so resented his father's absences and the hard work left to the children that he balked against religion and turned into a drinking, gambling scalawag who earned the reputation of driving the fastest horse in the township! Sometime after his marriage to Grandmother Lavina (Jamieson), however, he was dramatically converted at a revival meeting, and although he would never be the same again, his style of life was, in many ways, just as radical as before. Now he condemned "drink" as a tool of the devil and turned against gambling so much that one day he grabbed his children's game of Snakes and Ladders and threw it in the fire just because it was played with dice.

He took to studying his Bible fanatically, and was not above getting up in church to argue vehemently over certain points with the minister, much to the embarrassment of his wife and family. Unfortunately, his religious conversion did not cure him of a violent temper which, if provoked, was unleashed at whomever or whatever was at hand. Nevertheless, he had a boisterous, fun-loving side, and Lola, Carf, and Art have memories of happy times spent with him and Grandma.

I only recall seeing him once when he visited at our home after my grandmother died in Chilliwack, B.C., where they had retired. He allowed me to stand by his side while he shaved with a dangerous-looking straight razor, carefully watching himself in a fascinating fold-out mirror stand. Stroking off his beard, he talked to me in a most adult fashion, and because I was only six or seven I felt very honoured as he recounted experiences from his early life and told me about his first wife (before grandmother) who had died when she was very young. Later in his life, he married for the third time, but that marriage lasted only a few weeks, after which time he and his new wife discovered that they were completely incompatible. I suspect it was a great shock to Grandfather to find a woman with as strong a will and as unbending a character as his own.

Grandma Lavina looks out of her wedding picture a pretty but serious girl, and I seem to detect a little sadness in the eyes, which is not surprising. She had had a heartbreaking experience when her first love swept her off her feet, then broke his promises and left her pregnant when she was only seventeen. This was more than a hundred years ago and one can only imagine the scandal that swept the small rural community and the shame and torment endured by her and her parents. Nevertheless, her staunch Presbyterian, Scottish family stood solidly behind her and there was no thought of putting her baby up for adoption.

Grandma's sad experience had long-reaching effects. Many years later, when our own father drew up his last will, he left a small inheritance to his great-grandchildren born within a certain length of time, including "all great-grandchildren born, legitimate and illegitimate alike." Because of his deep sympathy and love for his mother, one of her small great-great granddaughters received an inheritance she might not otherwise have gotten.

Aunt Cora was the eldest in Dad's family, a quaint, bright-eyed little lady very much like Grandma Cann. She was a "sweetheart" loved by everyone, and was one of those rare and now seldom seen innocents who could scarcely bring herself to think badly of anyone. She married Uncle Charlie Densmore and lived all her life in Ontario on the original Cann homestead.

Uncle Lawrence, next in age to Aunt Cora, was a gentleman in every sense of the word, quiet and soft-spoken. Next to him came Alex (our father) and finally Uncle Art, who was always full of fun and jokes. It's not much wonder we children all adored him when we were little, the way he teased and made a fuss over us.

19

Dad's family: front, Grandma Lavina holding a neighbour's child, Aunt Cora, Grandfather Abram, and Uncle Art; back, Uncle Lawrence and Alex (Dad).

Because Dad was always so mild-mannered in both his words and actions, it was hard for me to believe he had once had a very bad temper. One day, when he and Uncle Art were children, they got into a violent fight in the barn. As older brothers are wont to do, he was teasing his little brother until the latter got so mad that he threw a pitchfork at him, spearing his bare big toe. The scare and the pain sent Dad berserk; he rushed at Art and beat him until he was senseless. Suddenly, Dad was sure he had killed Art, and sheer terror filled his heart. The understanding of what an uncontrolled temper could do washed over him sickeningly, and he vowed from that day on never to let his anger get the better of him.

It rarely did. I recall seeing him lose his temper on only two occasions, once at the boys when they disobeyed him and got into some serious trouble, and once when a balky horse took his patience to the ropes. Because his anger was so out of character, it was both shocking and bewildering. Mother's frequent bursts of rage could be shrugged off easily, but Dad's seldom-seen anger quelled the soul.

Dad had a conversion experience when he was twelve, but even before that he took his faith seriously. In our family Bible there is an old card signed in his childish eight-year-old hand and dated 1899. It reads:

> *I do hereby pledge myself to abstain from the use of all Alcoholic Liquors as a beverage, from the use of Tobacco in any form, from the use of Profane Language, the reading of Bad Books and Papers, and to earnest efforts to secure the Prohibition of Liquor Traffic.*

He kept his oath all the days of his life, and years later, when the doctor prescribed brandy for Mother's heart condition, it was an ordeal for him to frequent the liquor store. But because there was nothing he wouldn't do for Mother, he endured the embarrassment.

After his conversion, he secretly hoped to become a minister, but schooling did not come easily in those days and he was needed to work on the family farm after he finished elementary school. Although he wasn't able to reach his ambition, he lived his Christian faith every day of his life. How comforting it was for me as a child to tiptoe past his room and see him thoughtfully reading the Bible, or kneeling by the bedside in prayer. I was positive my dear father had a special line direct to God.

Half an hour or so before I was sent off to bed, I snuggled up in his lap while he read to me. Often it was one of Thornton W. Burgess' wildlife stories which ran as a serial in the *Saskatoon Star Phoenix*, and which we cut out and saved. I knew every antic of Peter Rabbit, Johnny Chuck, Prickly Porky, and all their other friends long before I could read. One Christmas, Santa Claus brought me an Uncle Wiggley book, and I laughed until I cried when Dad took on the deep voice of Uncle Wiggley or the nervous squeak of Nurse Jane. Although he must have gotten tired reading that book, he never refused me when I begged, "Please, read it again!"

Breaking up the land on Section 10 near Brock: Dad (back of steam engine) and a neighbour.

The Cann horses on show, about 1918.

While Mother was never enthralled by the West, Dad loved its wildness and revelled in pitting his rugged strength against the challenges it offered. He broke and tilled the land with the help of the beautiful Clydesdale horses he had brought from Ontario. He and Uncle Lawrence showed

21

them, the horses decked in fancy harness with gleaming brass, at many exhibitions, and won several ribbons and silver cups.

Although he was a strong man with deep faith, the difficult days of the 1930s took their toll. One night, when things were at their most desperate, when the crops had failed, when the mortgage payment was overdue, when Mother's nerves were raw and blinding headaches sent her to bed, when she talked of returning to her folks in Ontario, I awoke to the terrifying sound of my father crying. As his racking sobs filled the room, I froze in bed, sure that the end of the world had come. Then, as Mother whispered comfort, his crying gradually ceased, and although I couldn't catch their words, they talked into the dawn, when I finally fell back to sleep.

Next morning I was afraid to go downstairs, fearing the worst. Although their faces were calm, I was not reassured, feeling I was in the eye of a cyclone that would break at any moment. It never did. Whatever crisis had sparked my dad's deep tears (I suspect it was Mother's veiled threat to leave), it passed over, or was alleviated, and to my knowledge never arose again.

This experience had a lasting effect on me. At a very early age I realized that life could sometimes deal such terrible blows that even strong grown-ups like my dad could weep as if their very souls were being ripped apart.

A few years after this, he and Mother made the painful decision to leave Saskatchewan and make another start in Ontario. It was not easy to turn their backs on the farm into which they had poured so much of their energies and hopes for almost twenty-five years. At an age when many men think of retiring, Dad had the courage and the foresight to purchase a bankrupt business in Exeter, Ontario, and with the help of Carf and Art to build it into a thriving enterprise.

Politics interested him keenly. In Saskatchewan, he was a forceful proponent of the old CCF party, a supporter of J. S. Woodsworth and a cohort of J. M. Coldwell. Although he knew he hadn't a hope of winning in Tory Ontario, he nevertheless ran for parliament on the CCF ticket in 1944 because he believed its views should be put forth to the people. I was his twenty-one-year-old manager, enthusiastic but green!

Dad was loved by many and respected by everyone for his honesty and fair-mindedness. There were customers who sometimes ran up large accounts and who didn't appear to make much effort to pay them off. While my brothers urged him to "get tough" or sue, he rarely took that course. Because he remembered his own hard times during the Depression, he was inclined to take a softer, more lenient approach. He could never stop believing that people were basically good and honest; only a few let him down.

22

Because he did expect the best of you, you were inclined to give it to him, not wanting to disappoint him. But sometimes I did. When I was sixteen and living in Ontario, all the kids in my gang collected at the local hangout after school to drink Coke and smoke cigarettes. No one used tobacco in our family, not even my brothers, but I wasn't about to be different from the crowd and soon learned to blow smoke rings with the best of them. Initially, I smoked only at the restaurant with my friends, but soon I was bold enough to open my bedroom window and puff away while I studied. Since I always cleaned my own room, I felt safe in disposing the butts and ashes in my waste basket. It was my undoing. One day, on an overly zealous cleaning spree, Mother emptied my basket and found the damning evidence.

If Mother had been true to her character she would have come rushing at me with lusty accusations. But for some reason she turned the evidence over to Dad.

That evening, while she busied herself someplace else in the house, he accosted me quietly, "I hear you've taken up smoking."

Startled and defensive, I shot back, "Who says?"

"Your mother found ashes and butts in your waste basket."

"Oh." I hung my head, all bravado vanishing.

Finally he broke the long silence. "I'm really sorry. Smoking is a bad habit, not only dangerous to your health but very expensive." His face was filled with such disappointment I found it hard to meet his eyes.

"I had hoped none of this family would ever take up smoking," he continued quietly, "but, of course, I know once you come of age (twenty-one) you can do as you wish. If you choose to smoke then, I'll still be very sorry, but I will respect your decision." The silence deepened as I slumped in my chair.

"However, at this moment you are only sixteen, you are living in your mother's and my house, we are supplying you with all your needs, so we have the right to tell you that you cannot smoke." All this was spoken in his gentle voice — no condemnation, just a great sadness at my lack of wisdom and his painful duty of setting me straight. The thought that I might have lost his respect almost shattered me.

He patted my shoulder and left the room, and I never smoked another cigarette in my life.

There's no doubt about it. In his quiet, gentle, understanding way he was the person who most influenced my life. And the security of his love surrounded me and my brothers and sister until the day he died.

~

CHAPTER SIX

Marks of the Depression

N ot long ago, I heard radio commentator Peter Gzowski say that those who lived in Saskatchewan during the Depression of the 1930s bore the mark all their lives.

I'm sure that's true, although the extent of the imprint will depend on how old you were and what you were doing at the time. I was only a little girl, yet some of the memories of those days still haunt me. Mother and Dad didn't quarrel often, but when they did, it shattered me. Constant pressure over bad crops and lack of money was always the cause of these confrontations. One day while they argued angrily at the kitchen table, I sat listening behind the door, bewildered, frightened, and hurting to my soul at their harsh words. When they eventually left the room, the terrible ache in my stomach gave way to violent vomiting. To this day, the sound of people quarrelling upsets me, and for me to quarrel with someone is something I cannot face, not because I don't often disagree with others, but because fighting literally makes me ill. It's always easier to say nothing and walk away without confrontation, which, of course, is not the way to handle a situation either. But that's one of the marks that's on me.

The farmers carried the deepest imprint from the Depression. They were like Pharaoh of old, caught in a labyrinth of seven plagues — depressed prices, drought, wind, hail, grasshoppers, army worms, and jack rabbits — all of which made farming a discouraging uphill battle, and some farms were lost for the lack of just a little capital.

This impression stayed with Dad until the day he died: he could never be completely convinced that there was more than enough money, and it disturbed him greatly to see somebody "wasting" it. Although I was little more than a child during the Depression, I too am overly anxious and bothered by forebodings of financial insecurity. I keep remembering when there were no finances.

Dad's parents retired to the Fraser Valley in British Columbia in the 1920s, where they cultivated a large garden and small orchard. Since they often produced more than they could use or sell, sometimes they boxed up fruit and shipped it to us. This was a wonderful treat, and free except for the COD freight charges.

One day in the '30s, the CNR station agent, Fred Groz, phoned to say there were two crates of raspberries waiting for us. Our mouths began to water, but there was a small catch: the freight charges were $2.50.

Now, Dad didn't have 50 cents in his pocket, let alone $2.50, but some of the neighbours owed him money for butchering their steers at the beef ring. Art was hoisted up on his horse and told to ride over to one of these men to see if he could rustle up enough money to free our berries.

This neighbour, Elmer Wiley, an upright Christian gentleman, was affronted when my brother stated his errand. "Tell your father," he answered with quiet dignity, "he knows very well that when I have money I pay my debts. He doesn't have to send a boy to collect them."

Receiving that message, Dad wasn't very hopeful when he sent Art to another neighbour for the same purpose. His suspicions were right. There was no cash to be had.

Fearing the raspberries would spoil, he rode into town and spoke to the station agent. "Fred, I can't raise the $2.50 for the freight, so you take the berries and use them yourself."

Fred considered briefly. They *were* nice-looking berries. "O pshaw, Alex, you'll have the money some day. Take the berries and get out of here!"

When recounting this story, Dad admitted he'd been astounded because a station agent was bound never to let out freight unless the charges were paid, and he suspected Fred dug into his own pocket. In any event, Dad hustled in with the $2.50 as soon as he got some money in his hands.

Kindnesses such as this were typical throughout the Depression, neighbours sharing with neighbours, assisting and supporting each other every way they could. The friendships made in those days were cemented with a glue that never came unstuck. Each neighbour was important to the welfare of all the others, and because most of them had no relatives in the area, they were closer than brothers and sisters.

The storekeepers were also a special breed, staking the farmers until the next crop. The fact that the next crop might be very slim didn't seem to deter them from giving credit. In this present hard-nosed age, it's difficult to believe they didn't even charge interest on overdue accounts.

I suppose there were some debts that were never collected, but each fall Dad's chief objective was to hurry to the store with his first wheat cheque to settle his bill. One lean year he owed $800, a whopping amount in those days. "If the storekeeper hadn't given us credit, we might have starved," he impressed upon us.

Well, we didn't starve, but it certainly was a luxury if Mother happened to bring home a box of Corn Flakes from the store. Usually our morning cereal was wheat ground and mixed with rolled oats. Coffee was made, sometimes, by grinding wheat that had been roasted in the oven, and once Mother and her friend, Jessie Jickling, even tried making soda crackers. They weren't as crispy as the store-bought kind, but soaked in our hot soup they tasted just fine.

Mother was a wonderful baker and as long as she had a bag of flour and sugar in the house she could turn out light cakes, flaky biscuits, and marvellous white bread. She didn't spend money on yeast, but kept a jar of "mother of yeast" behind the stove where in the warmth it fermented and grew. Each baking yielded eight huge round loaves as light as a feather. Nearly every week she'd pull a loaf from the hot oven, slice off the brown crust, slather it with butter, and share it with whomever happened to be in the kitchen with her. Often it was I, and my mouth still waters at the memory of it. If the bag of flour was getting low, the cakes and biscuits might be omitted from her weekly baking, but we always had that wonderful bread!

We never went hungry, but our diet was sometimes limited and we had to work for our food. Throughout the drought we children hauled heavy pails of water from the well to laboriously spill it over the long rows of the garden. Whatever it produced — carrots, peas, beans, beets, a few tomatoes, black currants, or gooseberries — Mother canned in quart sealers and stored on shelves in the basement.

Mother loved horseradish. As soon as its first green shoots poked through the earth in the corner of our garden every spring, she sent Dad out to dig it up so she could grind it into relish.

One April day long before I started school, and when the snow had just melted, I spied some of these green shoots of horseradish coming through the wet ground. Thinking I would really surprise Mother, I dragged Dad's round-mouthed shovel from the granary and, sinking nearly to my ankles, I started to dig. It took a lot of puffing and effort to finally pry up a few precious roots. Anticipating Mother's delight, I ran to the house to present my treasure. I did not receive the expected commendation. Instead, one horrified look at my shoes heavy with mud, my dirty hands and filthy clothes, brought forth an angry tirade. I was crestfallen, and even after she discovered what I was offering in my muddy hands she still ordered me out to the back steps to clean off my shoes with a kitchen knife, and made me scrub up at the kitchen sink, clucking and scolding all the while.

But she did grind up the few roots I had worked so hard to dig up and mixed them with white sugar and vinegar to have with our supper. And as she piled the relish on a slice of cold roast beef, she relented enough to admit it tasted "real good." Dad gave me a slow smile and a wink across the table.

Not everyone thought her horseradish relish was a treat! She didn't dilute it with anything, so it was very hot and had to be eaten with great care. Because it was such a favorite of hers, she always had it on the table in a good-sized bowl. One day when our neighbours, the Salkelds, were visiting, Mr. Salkeld mistook it for cabbage salad. Loading up his fork, he put the whole thing in his mouth and swallowed it all at once. Immediately his face took on the red glow of a setting sun. He threw back his chair and rushed to the water pail, downing three or four dipperfuls before he cooled down sufficiently to mop his tears and gasp, "Gad, Woman, you might have warned me!" Mother couldn't answer — she was howling with laughter!

The water from our well was very rusty in colour, the iron content being extremely high. Our water pail and dipper, tea kettle and cooking pots were all lined with a coating of red rust. Visitors didn't care for our drinking water, but we all thought it tasted fine. What a time Mother had, though, trying to do her laundry with that red water. Although she had a washing machine run by a gasoline engine, made her own lye soap, and used lots of squares of blueing tied up in an old hankie in the rinse water, she was never happy with the colour of her wash.

While Mother looked forward to the first horseradish each spring, I waited for the rhubarb to push its fat, rolled-up leaves through the earth. It was always a great day when there were enough red stalks for the first pie, and while Mother washed them and cut them up into small pieces she gave me a short, tender stalk to dip in a little glass of sugar. I chewed on the end, getting a blend of sweet and sour which was sometimes so acid it made my jaws ache and my face screw up. Still, I always begged for more!

Everybody on a farm made butter in those days, and we were no exception. After Carf and Art milked the cows and lugged the heavy pails of foaming milk into the house, they cranked the milk through a separator which stood in the back porch. The milk ran out a long spout while the yellow cream flowed through another, and when the process was finished all the spouts, bowls, and other apparatus were taken apart to be washed meticulously and rinsed with scalding water. It wasn't a job I enjoyed.

The boys took the skim milk back to the barn to feed to the calves and pigs while Mother carried the cream to the basement where it was stored in the coolness. In about a week we would have collected enough to be poured into the old wooden churn. After the lid was screwed down tightly, we took turns pushing an iron handle back and forth, which sent the churn tumbling over and over, splashing the cream against its sides. It seemed a long time before the splashing finally turned to a soft thumping which announced that the butter had arrived. The buttermilk was drained off from a spigot at the bottom of the churn, leaving a soft white mass that Mother lifted out into a large wooden bowl to be mixed thoroughly with a bit of salt and yellow food colouring. Then she packed it into a thick brown crock covered with a dinner plate to be generously spread on her good white bread and biscuits.

In summer, we had more eggs than we could use, and since there was no sale for them they were left in the barn wherever the hens dropped them. We youngsters engaged in many an egg fight, and getting one down your back was incredibly awful, especially if it happened to be rotten. In winter, the hens stopped laying, so eggs were preserved in crocks filled with a slimy, jelly-like substance called waterglass. It worked fairly well, but by the time spring rolled around the eggs were always beginning to show their age.

Once the hens started to lay again we gorged ourselves on scrambled and fried eggs. One spring I came down with a case of hives the size of small plates, which the doctor said likely came from eating too many eggs. Since the hives were terribly itchy and almost driving me mad, he prescribed a dark brown ointment for Mother to rub on me from head to toe every evening before bed. It turned my skin a coppery colour so that I looked like an Indian, which I rather liked, but the vile smell of it kept me awake most of the night. Every morning until the hives disappeared I had to spend extra time at the dry sink trying to scrub off the stench before I left for school.

Mother raised a few roasting roosters and turkeys for sale and for ourselves on special occasions. In the winter, sides of pork hung frozen in the icy outer kitchen, and the beef ring kept us in fresh meat during the summer.

But there were years when grasshoppers or army worms joined forces with the drought to obliterate our garden along with the crops. The ugly grasshoppers, huge brown things, were everywhere, even hurling themselves through car windows, leaving trails of repulsive "tobacco" juice on our clothes and shoes.

One summer, the grasshopper population was so great that clouds of them swarmed down to attack the crops. The harried farmers tried bravely to hamper their onslaught by spreading a mixture of poison and sawdust around their fields. It was not very successful.

If grasshoppers were disgusting, army worms were loathsome. They advanced in hordes, eating every morsel of vegetation. Nothing stopped them. They crawled over every obstruction, and the house and screen doors writhed with their vile mass of green and black. Keeping in a straight line, they marched on, leaving trees and hedges barren, tender grain plants stripped, gardens plundered, and the farmers angry and discouraged.

That year, our diet would have been very limited had not the generous people of the East, who were feeling the pinch themselves, come to the rescue by shipping out freight cars of produce. Perhaps because Dad was known throughout the district for his honesty, he was chosen to look after an orderly distribution of the goods. A committee had decided that the families who were hardest hit and who had the most children would be given the first handouts.

The freight car contained bags of potatoes, onions, and turnips, bushels of apples, and home-canned fruit and jam. There were big yellow cheeses from Ontario and slabs of dry salted codfish from the Maritimes. Western women had no idea how to cook the fish and tried to fry it, with disastrous results. One jokester suggested that the slabs be laced up for snowshoes, which seemed a good idea until it was discovered that the fish was quite delicious steamed and served with a cream sauce.

One of the first men to arrive when the relief car was to be unloaded was much better off than most and had only one small child. Dad asked him to stand aside until the needier families picked up their share. Waiting impatiently, he grew more and more annoyed as he watched the pile diminish. When his turn finally came, there was only a bag of turnips left. Because he felt he had been treated unjustly, and although Father tried to placate him, he never spoke to Dad again. That was too bad, but that man's attitude was certainly the exception rather than the rule in those days.

There was one story Dad could hardly tell for laughing. At the height of the Depression, the banks loaned money to scarcely anyone, no matter how unblemished their record. It was said that bankers had ice in their veins, and they were not very popular in the community.

This particular year, the drought had been so extreme that hardly any potatoes had been grown in the West. And they were very expensive, about ten dollars per hundred, retail. A group of farmers banded together to purchase a freight-car load and sell them at cost. The community was canvassed to fill a car and the order sent off to Prince Edward Island.

Eventually, the potatoes arrived, but they couldn't be unloaded until COD was paid to the railway agent. Dad, who again was placed in charge, didn't have the money, nor did anyone else. So he paid a call on the young banker who had just moved to town. He told him the story of the potatoes, how they were all ordered and would be paid for as each farmer picked up his allotment, how he simply needed a loan for one day. The banker seemed to think it was a reasonable request and told Dad to make out the necessary cheque to the station agent and that he (the bank manager) would cover it until Dad came in with the money.

He forgot to ask the amount of money needed and Dad hadn't bothered to tell him, so later when the station agent brought in the cheque to be cashed and the banker saw it was for $2,500, he almost died of apoplexy. Apparently he had thought it would be two or three hundred dollars, and to take the risk of loaning $2,500 in those days would certainly be considered irresponsible by his superiors. He dashed out into the street trying to locate Dad, who by this time had been warned by the station agent that the banker was looking for him with blood in his eye. Because the man was so new in town and because he hadn't taken a good look at Dad when the agreement was made, he passed by him several times without recognizing him!

In any event, the potatoes were unloaded and all paid for, and at the end of the day Dad marched into the bank with all the cash to cover the loan. The young bank manager almost fainted with relief.

So yes, Peter Gzowski is right, the Depression did leave its mark, but I think that most of us who came up through it remember the good times even better than the bad. The beautiful, caring spirit of the adults in our lives — parents, neighbours, teachers, preachers, storekeepers — their indestructible sense of humour in the face of many troubles, left its imprint on us. It was a privilege to grow up among those people who showed us, by example, how to live life with courage and hope.

~

CHAPTER SEVEN

And the Wind Blew

T he Dirty Thirties! If you lived in Saskatchewan, they were dirty all right. By the time the years of drought came, the land had been overworked; the black topsoil that blew around invaded everything. Although we were part of the Palliser Triangle, the driest area, we didn't experience the most extreme drought conditions that the southern part of the province endured. Nevertheless, it was bad enough, and I assumed that the Depression had been caused by the drought and the big winds that lapped up our good rich soil like some huge, black, growling beast which spewed the earth out again to shroud the sun. As I have said before, to me the Depression meant (and still does), not the collapse of the stock market, but hot dry summers, failed crops, and roaring winds. I have some fearful memories of those awesome blows.

Usually, the dust storms started with a dark yellowish cloud on the western horizon, the cloud growing until it was over us with terrifying speed and noise. Barn and granary doors were battened down and the windows of the house hung with blankets before we dashed to the safety of the basement. The world grew dark and ominous as the near-cyclone winds whipped around the buildings, sending all kinds of debris careening through the air.

Finally, when all was calm again, we climbed up the stairs, to be met with dust piled everywhere. Even the heavy blankets covering the windows couldn't keep it out. Mother would sigh, thankful the damage wasn't worse, push up her sleeves and put us children to work with brooms and dustpans while Dad ventured outside to check the outbuildings, animals, and crops. Although there sometimes was damage to buildings, it was the crops that suffered most. Often, it seemed, the winds hit just after the seed had been planted or before the tiny plants had a foothold to endure the force of those terrible blows and cutting sand. And another crop would be lost.

It was a horrific experience to be caught out in one of those storms. Visibility was often cut to zero and the black sand stung your face as it lashed into your eyes and nose. Once, when Art and Carf were on their way to a baseball game in Kindersley, a dust storm broke upon them. The telephone poles and ditches faded from their view, making it impossible to see where they were going. Turning off the motor, they prepared themselves to wait out the wild darkness that surrounded them.

Eventally, as the winds abated, the dust began to settle and the air to clear. To their astonishment, a car was facing them on the road, its hood no more than a foot from their own. Neither they nor the occupants of the other car had been aware that the others were there throughout the storm.

I recall another family being caught in one of these storms on the highway about half a mile from our place. They were in an old touring car, and the flimsy canvas and mica curtains didn't afford much protection from the dirt that blasted in from every side. When the winds passed over, they straggled into our yard, visibly shaken and looking like minstrel-show castaways with red-rimmed eyes peering from dust-blackened faces.

Another time I was visiting with Viola and Ernie Hyde, favorites with all the neighbourhood children, when a violent storm lunged over us with such speed that we didn't even have time to close the kitchen window. Viola and I had been preparing a picnic lunch of fancy sandwiches and devilled eggs when Ernie had rushed in and unceremoniously pushed us through the trap door to the basement. There had been no time to bring the dog, and we could hear him whining and pacing madly above us. Ernie was about to lift the door to rescue him when a deafening crash shook the whole place. We dove under the steps, huddling together, fearing the house would come down.

It didn't, and when the winds calmed we went up to view the damage. The dog was safe back in the farthest corner under a bed, but our beautiful lunch was unrecognizable under an inch of black dirt. Most spectacular of all was the back porch, lifted by the wind and perched drunkenly on the roof of the small frame house. I remember how we laughed, I think from sheer relief that the crash we'd heard hadn't caused more damage.

For me, it was always a frightening experience to crouch in the dark basement waiting for the winds to cease. It was only the adults' quiet strength and calmness that kept me from being utterly terrified. One day, however, I had to brave it out on my own.

As I returned from school, I noticed the foreboding clouds forming up in the west. I ran to the house, but Mother wasn't there. Dashing to the barn and calling frantically for Dad, I received no answer. Panic rose in my throat as the realization dawned that I was going to have to face this storm alone.

The roar of the relentless wind filled my ears as the black clouds bore down, sucking up the parched earth. As frightened as I was to stand there in the middle of the yard and watch the storm bear down on me, I was still more terrified to turn and run into the basement and stay there by myself.

The huge dark clouds rolled closer and closer, obliterating the view of the neighbour's farm. Trembling from head to foot, heart pounding in my small chest, I squeezed my eyes tight and prayed with a fervor unknown to me before, "Oh, God, *please* help me!"

I opened my eyes. The roaring dust clouds, which a few moments before had been moving straight for our buildings, suddenly veered off to the north and skirted the place. My shaking knees let me down to the ground.

Sometimes I still taste the terror of watching that approaching storm. But I can also feel the happy surprise and deep gratitude for a frightened little girl's answered prayer. That was the beginning of a new, friendlier relationship between God and me. But I still don't like big winds.

~

Chapter Eight

On Stage!

I n 1928, a year before the Depression struck, Dad bought a new car, a classy blue Chevrolet with nickel trim and glass windows that wound up and down, a great improvement over the mica curtains stored under the back seat of the touring car he'd purchased the year I was born (1923). If a sudden rainstorm came up while we were out driving in that old car, there was always the scurry of getting the curtains domed up along the sides before we were soaked to the skin. Also, to get the engine going someone had to stand at the front and crank it up while another person pulled and pushed the choke and gas knobs on the dashboard. It could be balky, and sometimes the "cranker" got quite a kick when it backfired. In fact, more than one person had an arm broken that way. By comparison a floor starter pressed by the foot got the motor in the new car humming easily. We were thrilled to our toes when Dad, grinning from ear to ear, drove it into the yard because we knew it was the absolute ultimate in modern transportation.

After purchasing this new automobile, Dad ripped out the back seat of the old car, replacing it with a homemade wooden box to turn it into a small makeshift truck. It came in handy for many chores, including picking up grain sheaves in the fields and taking them to the barn to feed the animals. I learned to drive this little old truck when I was about six. Perched on a pile of gunny sacks so I could see over the steering wheel, I manoeuvred from stook to stook while Dad pitched on the sheaves — and don't think I didn't feel important!

As I say, the little truck was very useful. The boys drove it to the many Sports Days where they played baseball, and it was used on the farm in innumerable ways, hauling wheat to the flour mill twenty miles away or water to the cattle in the municipal pasture. But as far as I was concerned, the truck's box rendered its best service as a stage for the many performances I put on for a make-believe crowd.

Sometimes I danced for them, weaving in and out of one of Mother's old scarves. Other times I acted out plays that I made up as I went along. The audience was always appreciative, and my ears rang from their clapping and cheers as they called me back for encore after encore. Of course I had to be very careful that my big brothers weren't within hearing distance, for they liked nothing better than to interrupt my act with jeering and cat-calls.

I suppose my fascination with the theatre came from the Tent Chautauqua, a touring theatrical company that crossed the West every year. I don't remember my first Chautauqua because I was carried in my father's arms, but I do know that as I grew older I waited for Chautauqua with as much excitement as Christmas. What a day it was when the big brown tent was hoisted up on the fairgrounds next to the rink. We all trooped in to sit on hard wooden seats with the dry earth under our feet and the smell of the canvas tent in our nostrils, completely spellbound by the performances.

By the time I was five or six I had seen many plays, including *Here Comes Charlie*, *Uncle Tom's Cabin*, and *The Importance of Being Ernest*. There were also shows featuring sleight-of-hand artists, jugglers, dancers, opera singers, violinists, elocutionists, and profound lecturers on many subjects.

Chautauqua lasted one short week, cost about ten dollars a family, and was sheer magic from beginning to end. How sad I was when this cultural institution faded into history because the Depression allowed no money for such luxury.

However, we still had our battery-run radio. Dad made very sure it was "charged up" for Saturday night when two of his friends often joined him for *Hockey Night in Canada* broadcast from Toronto. These men were Joe Salkeld, an Englishman who fought in the Great War, and Dick Heede, a German soldier on the other side. Both emigrated to Saskatchewan and became fast friends because they knew no matter what side you were on, war was a senseless tragedy. Each sat on the edge of his diningroom chair, gallantly cheering on the Toronto Maple Leafs and lifting two feet in the air with whoops of joy when Foster Hewitt yelled, "He shoots, he scores!"

While the Saturday night broadcasts were engrossing for the grownups, it was the late afternoon shows that held my rapt attention. Sitting on a small stool with my ear close to the speaker, I listened to the spine-tingling episodes of *Little Orphan Annie, Jack Armstrong, the All American Boy,* and *Cecil and Sally*, a story about two love-stricken young people. In the evenings, there was the *Lux Radio Theatre* starring famous movie actors: Amos and Andy, Eddie Cantor, comedians Jack Benny and Mary Livingstone, George Burns and Gracie Allen, Fibber McGee and Mollie. What a feast of entertainment it was.

Another enthralling diversion was the Christmas Tree Concert put on by the schoolteachers and pupils. Since the auditorium of the United Church was the largest in the community, the concert was performed in the raised chancel lit by the white light of mantle lanterns. Dark shadows fell over the intent audience, but over in the corner beside the chancel a breathtakingly magnificent pine tree shone through the darkness with yards and yards of silver tinsel, brightly coloured chains, and gleaming glass ornaments. As far as I can remember it was the only Christmas tree in the district and was a marvellous, mystical spectacle that sent shivers through my small bones.

Before I started school I listened to Carf, Art, and Lola practising their parts and songs until by the night of the concert I knew them as well as they did. The first Christmas concert I remember I sat on Mother's knee, completely entranced while Lola and two friends, all about thirteen, tripped around the stage singing "In My Sweet Little Alice Blue Gown." Mother had spent hours sewing Lola's dress of blue satinized cotton with large petals forming the skirt and trimmed with yellow posies. Watching my big sister performing on the stage made me proud beyond measure and I thought she was the most beautiful thing I'd ever seen! The same night, I laughed and clapped as Carf and Art in tattered pants and old jackets, ragged caps pulled down over their ears and bundles tied up in big red hankies on the end of sticks, bellowed "Hallelujah, I'm a Bum."

When I started school I was eager to take part in these concerts, but during my very first performance, while singing "I've a Dear Little Dolly, She's Got Eyes of Bright Blue," I looked out on a *real* audience and was petrified. Unable to control my nervousness, I slowly twisted up the hem of my dress until a good part of my underpants was showing. There were titters in the audience, and Art and Carf teased me about it for weeks.

As I grew older, I conquered most of the nervousness, and always hoped the teacher would pick me for a "good" part in one of the plays. How disappointed I was when, in Grade 7, I was selected to play the piano for the operetta, *Windmills of Holland*, when all I wanted was to be up on the stage *acting*. When I was about eleven, Lola took me to see my first movie, Disney's *Snow White and the Seven Dwarfs*. While I was captivated by the animated cartoon characters, I was a little disappointed that they weren't real actors with whom I could identify!

It was Chautauqua, radio programs, and Christmas concerts that fed my imagination so that I dreamed of becoming a famous actress. That never happened, of course. Nevertheless, in my younger years I was involved with amateur theatre and still have the silver plate I

The Windmills of Holland *cast and crew. I'm shown kneeling in front with my friend Mary Krepps, who turned the pages for me as I played the piano.*

won for "most promising actress" at a drama festival adjudicated by the now well-known director, Leon Major. I still love to see a good performance.

When I watch my little grandchildren twirling round on their toes and putting on "shows," my mind always goes back to the small child who performed so earnestly on the back of her dad's old truck. It strikes me that even when not on a real stage I've been acting most of my life, as I'm sure many people do — sometimes just to survive. I've laughed when I felt like crying, and cried when I felt no pain. And there are still days when I feel like an actor who hasn't read the script, who doesn't understand the play, but who is asked to perform anyway.

Shakespeare says all of life is a stage, and I like that analogy. There are times, to our credit, when we do act with some talent and finesse, but unfortunately there are also occasions when we miss our cue, blunder, and make complete fools of ourselves. When at our best, we can turn in a performance as noble as St. Joan's, but when our moods are devious we are also capable of turning out an act that would rival Lady McBeth's. And sometimes we feel we're playing the part of Orphan Annie, lost and alone.

So yes, we all act on life's stage, but even though we may feel ill-equipped and unrehearsed, and that the script is quite beyond our comprehension, I've learned that we don't need to be up there crashing about hopelessly and blindly. God is our Director, and He's always up front cuing us in. We must have faith in what He's doing, and be quiet enough to hear His directions.

~

CHAPTER NINE

Beautiful Dolls, Sad Events

hen I grew tired of playing with my imaginary friends or putting on plays in the back of the truck, I picked up my dolls and went to my playhouse, which was not a "house" at all but a very special place in the grove of soft maples that surrounded our large garden. Down among the low, spreading branches of the small trees, I found a secluded spot that was perfect for playing house. With an old blanket spread for a bed, two wooden orange crates for cupboards, a few broken dishes, and my dolls, I whiled away many hours as the leaves rustled gently above me.

I suppose because Mother had had such a lovely playhouse when she was a child, she thought I should fix up the empty van for mine. It was a box-like winter vehicle made of canvas and wood and pulled over the snow on sleighs by a team of horses. During the summer it stood unused, resting idly beside a granary. Sometimes I did play in it, but I much preferred my secret bower in the trees where I put on tea parties and sang lullabies to my dolls.

My first doll was Baby Jean, given to me when I was born by our closest neighbours, Mr. and Mrs. Berrow. The doll had a china head, a soft cuddly body, painted-on brown hair, and tiny blue eyes that smiled above chubby cheeks. Baby Jean was my most prized possession for years.

I loved Mr. and Mrs. Berrow too, and visited them often, chattering away and sipping tea at the round table in their cluttered diningroom. Mrs. Berrow always served green tea, something Mother disdained and wouldn't have in the house but which I thought was delectable. The Berrows' place was fascinating. The neat white frame house sat beside a small dam dug out by Mr. Berrow and surrounded by shiny-leaved poplar trees; it was

38

probably as close to an English setting as this British couple could achieve on the prairies.

They used only three small rooms of the house, the kitchen, diningroom, and bedroom, but there was another mysterious part that was closed off and never opened to view. According to Mother, it contained a large livingroom complete with piano and other fine furniture, and had been shut off when the Berrows' sixteen-year-old daughter, Alice, died suddenly of spinal meningitis. This happened before my memory, but Mother's description of the event was forever etched on my mind. Alice, a sweet, talented girl with long brown hair, was loved by everyone, and because Mother was enraptured over her wonderful qualities, Alice became in my childish mind half-princess, half-angel.

The community was shocked when she took suddenly and fatally ill. Mother sat with the distraught parents, applying cold cloths to the poor girl's head, which was bursting with pain, until she died. The doctor was afraid the disease was infectious so wouldn't allow Mother to return to her own family until she had disinfected her body and clothes. He also asked Dad to perform the sad act of destroying Alice's faithful little kitten, which was sleeping on the bed when she died. It was Dad, too, who gently wrapped the young

Alice Berrow.

girl's body in a sheet and lovingly laid it in the wooden coffin that he and another neighbour had constructed for a hurried burial.

The death of their young daughter deeply affected the woe-stricken Berrows. In fact, Mother said they were never the same again. Alice's name was never mentioned, and because they couldn't bear to look at her bedroom and the livingroom with the piano she loved, they closed them off.

When I was old enough to visit the Berrows, these unused rooms intrigued me, and with my high imagination I fancied them very grand and palatial, holding all kinds of beautiful things. One day, when my curiosity could no longer be sustained, I ventured to ask Mrs. Berrow if I could have a peek. After a moment's hesitation, she unlocked the door between the diningroom and the livingroom and invited me to step inside. As my eyes wandered around the semi-darkened room, I saw that it was nowhere near as large as I had supposed, and the dusty furniture looked very ordinary. The only bit of elegance was the blue and white embossed wallpaper, which was turning yellow and beginning to peel.

Sad to say, the friendship between the Berrows and us was interrupted when Mother took great offense at something Mrs. Berrow said about one of my brothers. While Mother was never the least bit tardy in pointing out our faults herself, her loyalty to the family would not permit her to accept any criticism of us from someone else. She was incensed, and decreed that the Berrows' place was henceforth out of bounds for all of us. I couldn't believe it. In fact, I couldn't stand it for long. A few weeks later, I left the house when Mother wasn't looking and ran across the field to the Berrows' house. Answering my timid knock, Mrs. Berrow's face lit up. "Why Jack!" she called to Mr. Berrow, "Look here, it's Gwyneth." Immediately the kettle was put on and the green tea steeped. Soon we were sitting around the table sipping away like old times.

I dreaded going home to meet Mother's wrath but she was not as angry as I had expected. And when I continued to sneak away to take tea with my dear friends, she gave up and said nothing.

I'm sure both she and Mrs. Berrow were sorry that the friendship was broken, but both were too proud to take the first step toward reconciliation. Fortunately, some years later they did, more or less, make up, but what a pity that a friendship that had seen many good times and had withstood the tragedy of death had a blot put on it.

I suppose the Berrows took the place of the grandparents I never knew. In any event, I loved them deeply, and the doll, Baby Jean, they gave me.

I received another doll when I was about six or seven from Grandma Cann. It still sits on my what-not, a small slim doll about ten inches high with a china head, long braided hair, and glassy, deep blue eyes. She never had a name; I always just called her "Grandma's doll."

She came to me one Christmas when times were tough, when there wasn't much money for gifts. Knowing this, Grandma sent the doll to Mother with instructions to put it in my stocking from Santa Claus. To keep the secret, Mother carefully hid it in the far recesses of a high shelf in the pantry.

One day shortly after, while Mother was doing her Christmas baking, I became bored and, as any curious child might, began to rummage around in all the cupboards looking for something to amuse me. By standing tiptoe on the counter of the cupboard, I discovered I could reach into the farthest corner of the top shelf of the pantry. Since we kept only unused junk there, imagine how I gasped with amazement when I pulled out this dark-haired beauty in a red silk dress. I was positive that somehow this lovely doll had been placed there years before and been forgotten.

Wanting to share this marvellous discovery with my mother, I scrambled down and ran to tell her, the doll cradled in my arms. Of course, I expected her to be as overcome with joy as I was, so when she angrily snatched the doll from me and scolded me for being a naughty, snoopy girl, I ran to my bed and cried bitterly. It was years before I understood her deep disappointment at my finding the doll with which she so dearly wanted to surprise me on Christmas morning, and why she reacted the way she did.

Well, the doll was in my stocking, not as a present from Santa but from my grandmother. But the thrill of receiving her was gone. Perhaps that's the reason I never played with her, or perhaps it was because Grandma died soon after, and I put the doll away in the trunk for a keepsake.

Next to Baby Jean, the doll that gave me the most delight was Bubbles (called after my best friend) and I'm sure Mother got as much pleasure out of me receiving her as I did. About two years after the "Grandma doll" incident, she and Isabelle Clendening took the train to Saskatoon for a day's holiday and some shopping. They were the best of friends. Isabelle and her husband Earl lived on a farm one mile west of us, and the families were very close, always spending Christmas and New Year's together.

The Clendenings suffered a terrible tragedy when their eldest little son, Donald, disappeared one day. After hours of frantic searching, the distraught father discovered the small body in the watering trough. The parents were both heartbroken, but Isabelle was nearly crazed with grief. After the melancholy funeral, she and her eighteen-month-old baby, Claude, spent hours with Mother, who with her deep sympathy and understanding helped to restore her grief-stricken friend's emotional health. At that time, they were both pregnant, and in a few months I was born, with Jean (her dad nicknamed her Bubbles) making it on the scene six weeks later. A sister, June, completed the Clendening family two years after that.

Isabelle and Mother usually raised a few dozen turkeys and sold them in the fall. The extra money meant a day in the city to browse through stores

41

and take lunch at a nice restaurant. They always brought us children a small gift, so we waited expectantly for their return on the evening train.

On this particular occasion, Dad met Mother at the station, and after they drove into the yard she came into the house carrying a long mysterious box, her lovely face lit with a smile. I'm sure she originally intended to keep what was in the box until Christmas, but couldn't possibly hold such an exciting secret that long. So, placing the box on the diningroom table, she turned to me with shining eyes. "Open it," she said.

I lifted the lid timidly and was dumbfounded at what I saw lying in the layers and layers of crushed pale blue tissue paper: the most beautiful doll in the world, dressed in a pink frilly dress, with long golden curls showing beneath a matching bonnet. Her little feet were encased in ribbed white silk socks and tiny black patent leather shoes. Brown lashes sweeping across her rosy cheeks hid her blue eyes, but she smiled at me in her sleep with red lips slightly opened to reveal two white teeth and the tip of a tiny pink tongue. She was beyond my wildest dreams, and I could only stand transfixed with disbelief.

Mother was delighted with my reaction, but since she had given me the doll I was supposed to receive for Christmas it did create a problem. Certainly there was no money to spend on another gift, but when I awoke

Claude and Donald Clendening, taken shortly before Donald's tragic drowning.

on Christmas morning, there, spread out on the diningroom table, was a wardrobe of clothes for my beloved new doll. There were black and red pyjamas, a black coat and hat, and a red dress. I was delighted, but when Mother insisted they were all from Santa Claus, I couldn't help wondering aloud why they were made out of the same cloth as one of my sister's old dresses. Mother assured me that it would not be at all impossible for Santa to have some of the same material, and when I saw that Bubbles Clendening

42

received the same set of clothes for her new doll my mind was put to rest.

Because I prized my beautiful doll so much and because Mother impressed upon me that she had cost an enormous sum (three dollars), I took the best possible care of her, carefully brushing her hair and giving her dry baths because a wet one might have washed off her colour and made her cloth body soggy. I even pretended to feed her from my small, flat breast! And of course I always saw that she got the proper amount of sleep.

This almost turned out to be the end of her. One day I put her and Baby Jean down for their afternoon nap in my leafy outdoor playhouse and then forgot all about them until I was awakened in the night by the sounds of an approaching thunderstorm. As the lightning flashed and the wind blew

The Clendening trio: June, Bubbles (Jean), and Claude, about 1939.

against the house, I sat up in bed, panicking because my precious dolls were lying unprotected among the trees. I knew if I roused Dad for help that Mother would wake up too, and scold me for my carelessness. There was no use asking Art and Carf, sound asleep in the next room, because even if I did manage to wake them they'd probably tell on me.

There was nothing to do but make the rescue myself. Creeping down the dark stairs, I found my way to the back door. The wind tore at my nightgown and almost blew me off my feet. It hadn't started to rain, but the lightning was flashing closer and closer as the thunder crashed above my head. Gathering all my courage, I flew across the eerie yard down the small knoll to the maple trees, and as the wildly waving branches reached out for my hair and nightgown I scooped up the dolls and raced back to the house, heart thumping. Back up the stairs I crept and into my bed where I nestled down with a doll on either side just as the sky opened up.

I never did distress Mother by telling how close my dolls had come to ruin. She loved beautiful dolls all her life, and when she was in her seventies dressed dozens of them in intricate fairytale gowns or in costumes from other lands. Even today, I never see a lovely doll without remembering Mother.

~

CHAPTER TEN

Lifeline of Letters

L etters from home were the lifeline that kept Mother afloat during the years she was often swamped with homesickness. How she waited for the mail, pouring over every line from her mother and sisters with homey bits of gossip — who had a new baby, who had married, or was sick, or returning to health — all the little happenings that kept her in touch with a community she wouldn't see again for many years. Often there were enclosures — snapshots, newspaper clippings, seeds for her prairie garden, and sometimes even bits of cloth to go with a description of a sister's new outfit.

Letters could bring sad news too. Sometimes they arrived with envelopes edged in black to announce someone's demise. I remember the day Mother received one of these bringing the tidings of her own mother's death. It seems strange, now, that someone didn't telephone the news or at least send a telegram. But this was at the beginning of the Depression, and I suppose it would have been considered folly to spend money in such a fashion. In any event, the black-edged letter arrived days after the funeral, delivered by a neighbour who had picked up our mail in town.

Lola, Carf, and Art were at school and Dad was in the fields, so Mother and I were alone. Wondering why her hands were trembling, I watched anxiously as she slowly sat down in the kitchen rocking chair to open the envelope. Reading silently, she didn't lift her eyes from the pages until she had finished. Then, folding the letter and returning it to its envelope, she pushed it down deep in the big pocket of her apron. Brushing her hair from her forehead, she said softly, "Your Grandmother Hammond has died." Except for a slight twitch at the corner of her mouth, her face remained calm.

I had never seen my maternal grandmother. She was just a rather stern-looking lady peering from an old photograph in my parents' room, so I didn't feel all that remorseful. Still, something in my mother's dark eyes signified that I should play very quietly while she went back to shaping loaves of bread for the week's baking.

Later, when Dad came in from the barn for supper, I ran to tell him the news with childish innocence, "Grandma Hammond died!" One startled look from him was all that was needed to break Mother's dam of tears. She fled to the bedroom, Dad following to comfort her, while I was left alone in the kitchen, feeling somehow guilty and not fully able to understand the depth of her grief and loneliness. Sometimes in the following days she'd take me on her lap and we'd rock back and forth for hours in the old chair.

This was Mother's favorite chair; she even pulled it up to the table to eat her meals, and she often sat in it cuddling Dimples, her big, black, pampered Persian cat. She had seen Dimples in a pet store on one of her Saskatoon excursions and couldn't resist his kitten charms. He came home with her in a box on the train, a tiny bit of black fluff that grew into an immense cat. She loved him and talked to him as if he were a baby, spoiling him beyond measure and even excusing his idiosyncrasy of nipping her nose with his sharp teeth when she became too amorous and hugged him too tightly.

It was in the big old rocking chair, too, that she composed letters to her children when they went off to Normal School in Saskatoon. Although Dad was always busy, he usually scratched a few lines of advice, wisdom, or humour on the bottom of Mother's last page, adding "ha, ha" after the humour just in case his offspring weren't quite smart enough to catch the joke.

Mother made it known in no uncertain terms that she expected a letter every week in return. When the letters arrived, she tore them open, savouring the tales of discovery and accomplishment, and sorrowing over failures and disappointments. These letters were dug out from her apron pocket, unfolded, read time and again, and discussed in detail at the supper table.

Farm kids away from everything that was familiar had plenty to write home about — new friends, eccentric teachers, class projects and social events, and of course the food at the boarding house. How Mother chortled when Art, a wholesome lad with a good appetite, wrote, "Am almost dying for a thick slab of roast beef and a big slice of your lemon pie, Mom; I'm getting mighty sick of creamed peas and toast!" The next time he came home for a weekend he was greeted with a steaming roast of beef and a lemon pie three inches thick.

Mother wrote letters to her relatives and friends almost all her life, but because she and Dad seldom parted, few epistles passed between them.

When Mother was in the hospital a short time before her death, however, Dad wrote her one last letter. He started out with news of the children and grandchildren and comments about the garden and weather. He told her: "The house is awfully lonely and dull without you even though you might be considered a nuisance to me sometimes (ha, ha)." And ended: "Rest assured my darling, darling wife, my love for you is as strong as it was 60 years ago," and then he thanked God for the devotion, faith, and years they had shared and spent together.

It was the last of the many letters Mother received in her lifetime, to be unfolded over and over, read and reread to gather comfort, joy, and strength.

Our house on the prairie as it was in the 1930s. In the summertime, Mother grew plants in the closed-in veranda. The small building on the right was used only in the warm weather; during the winter, our meat hung there to freeze. In my mind I can still walk through every room in this house, see every stick of furniture, and hear the creak of Mother's rocking chair.

~

CHAPTER ELEVEN

Brock Brick School

Mother thought the ride to school was too long for me, especially in winter, so she didn't send me off until I was almost seven. I was so excited that September morning I couldn't stop wiggling as she struggled to put on my socks, until she gave me a sharp slap on the leg. I pouted and thought it terribly unkind of her to spoil my first day at school by being so cross, but this was 1930 when the Depression was afflicting everyone's life, and I suspect that Mother was worried about something or other, as she often was in those days. The day I started school, Lola, at the age of seventeen, was commencing her teacher's training in Saskatoon and I'm sure Mother's concern was with her, too.

If I considered Mother unkind, I was almost overwhelmed by the kindness of Miss Veum, my first teacher. She was a sweet lady, gentle, soft-spoken, who made each child feel special. Her dark brown hair was pulled back smoothly and she wore a rose silk scarf tied in a bow at her neck, the scarf accenting the softness of her face. Instantly I was her slave.

She taught Grades 1, 2, and 3 in the lower room of the Brock Brick School, the one built in 1912. This building had only one other room, which was on the upper level along with a small laboratory. When it was erected, the school was plenty large enough to hold all the children, but as the area was settled the student population grew to overflowing. Consequently, by my time, classes had spread out into three buildings, the original school, an unused frame country school, drawn up at its side and always referred to as the "White School," and the village hall, which had originally been the Presbyterian church. All high school grades were taught in the upper room of the main building by the principal, Mr. MacArthur. Grades 4, 5, and 6 were in the White School while Grades 7 and 8 were in the hall. Hence there were four teachers for twelve grades, and they felt fortunate to be in a consolidated school rather than in some far-flung country school where they would

The Brock Brick School, the coal house, and the White School. Two grades met in the village hall.

have to teach all the elementary grades and perhaps Grade 9 and 10 as well.

For the most part, we had good teachers dedicated to their profession and students, and our curriculum certainly covered much more than reading, writing, and arithmetic. Besides the regular subjects of English, Geography, History, Mathematics, and Social Studies, we were instructed in many of the social graces — how to make a proper introduction, how to set a formal table, the etiquette of eating — and even the boys learned how to mend a sock, sew on a button, and do a few simple stitches. Though there were no symphony orchestras nor museums for hundreds of miles, the music and art appreciation classes stimulated our interest and gave us our first glimpse into a far-off world.

After lunch, in the lower grades, the teacher always read a chapter or two from a book. It was a spellbinding time that introduced us to Robinson Crusoe, Big Red, The Swiss Family Robinson, Black Beauty, Captain Red Ready, Huckleberry Finn, Beautiful Joe, and a host of other enchanting characters hitherto unknown to us. It was the best time of the day for me.

Our school sports equipment was negligible, but most of us were still enthusiastic athletes. There was a basketball for the older girls, who all tried to make the "first" team so they could compete against the teams at D'arcy and Netherhill, towns to the east and west of Brock. There always seemed to be a teacher skilled in the game to coach us with *esprit de corps*.

For the boys there was a baseball and a bat or two, but they had to bring their own mitts to take part in their ballgames. Hardball in Saskatchewan at that time was taken very seriously and produced many excellent players who competed in tournaments across the province.

The small children spent recess playing Hop Scotch, Scrub, or games like Run, Sheep, Run and Red Light. In the winter we congregated in the basement for In and Out the Windows and London Bridge is Falling Down. There were two small rooms, one for the boys and one for the girls. When outdoors, we all played together, but for some reason there was a rule that we could not go into each other's rooms in the basement. Only a very brave boy would take up the dare of his mates to run brazenly through the girls' room while we all screeched like a bunch of chickens and raced upstairs to "tell" the teacher. Those rooms were dark, with scarcely any light coming in the small windows, and the smell of carbolic acid from the indoor toilets was often overpowering, but the rooms were warm and provided a place for us to let off steam in the cold weather.

Some of the older boys held a kind of secret club in the furnace room when the janitor, Bill Melville, wasn't around. They kept a guard at the closed door and used a password, and we little children thought they were doing "bad" things in there, but I suspect now it was all very innocent.

Bill Melville and his wife, Belle, who kept the school clean, put up with a good deal of nonsense from the boys, who teased them unmercifully and played jokes on them until Belle, with a hot Scottish temper, would lace into them with her tongue and sometimes with a broom, her eyes blazing fire. Nevertheless, there was great affection for the Melvilles, and school would not have been nearly as interesting without slow-moving Bill and his peppery little wife.

Our annual school field day was probably the most important event of the year. We competed against all the other schools in the area which, counting the country schools, was quite a number, and for weeks we practised every recess. First we had to learn how to march in an orderly fashion, so every morning Mr. MacArthur lined us up in straight rows according to grades and marched us around the edge of the schoolyard while he shouted, "Left, right, lef-t, he had a good job and he lef-t, he lef-t, he had a good job and he lef-t."

On field day all the schools marched proudly, carrying their banners, and the school judged the best received a coveted prize, perhaps five dollars, to buy sports equipment. There were many events: running, high jumping, broad jumping, relay races, ball throwing, baseball, and basketball, to name some. My prowess was in broad jumping and running. Being naturally swift of foot, I easily won all the races until I was about ten, and then I got a terrible shock when, as I was confidently coasting along, a girl from another school overtook and passed me! From then on I had to work hard at my running, and it was always a close match between her and me. But nobody could ever beat me at broad jumping. One year I even went on to win a silver medal in a larger provincial event. (It's always been a source of amusement and, maybe, embarrassment, to my family that I won my highest honours in broad jumping!)

School was a happy time for me, and I made many good frineds, one of whom was Annie Kachmarski. She was from a large Ukrainian family that lived south of Brock, and since we lived to the north she and I had no contact until we met at school. Annie was a raw-boned, rather awkward, poorly dressed girl with straight brown hair and a big beautiful smile who loved to dance. Every noon hour we pushed the desks to the centre of the room and she tried to teach me some steps. We had no music so we had to sing, and I can still see us flying around the room trilling breathlessly, "Heel, toe, and away we go. Heel, toe, and away we go. Heel toe and away we go. Heel toe and away we go. La, la, laa, la la la, laa. La, la. Laa, la, la, la, laa. La, la, laa, la la, la, laa, heel, toe, and away we go!"

I was very fond of Annie and would have liked her for a close friend, but when I suggested to Mother that I invite her home for a night she discouraged the idea because she said Annie's family might have bedbugs. Now, if there was anything Mother had declared war on it was bedbugs. Apparently they were quite prevalent in the early days, and to Mother's horror the old settler's shack she and Dad had pulled alongside our house for a summer kitchen had been infested. She never ceased to impress upon us how hard she had scrubbed and disinfected to get rid of them, and she wasn't about to take any chances on getting them again. Whenever we visited a place she wasn't sure about, she went over our clothes with a fine-toothed comb when we came home, just in case we'd picked up a bug.

Once, Art did bring one or two home, which sent Mother into a flurry of scrubbing with formaldehyde and scouring out every tiny crack of the boys' room. Another time, when one of Lola's friends, Marjorie Allen, a nurse, was working at a home not far from us, she came to our house directly her case was finished. "Oh, Mrs. Cann," she cried, "I've picked up bedbugs." Mother flew into the fray. All Marjorie's clothes were pulled from her suitcase, sprayed with formaldehyde, and hung out in the hot sun. She was given a bath and had her head and hair thoroughly washed before she was declared free of the infestation.

There's no doubt about it, bedbugs were a pest nobody wanted. They were prolific little beasts that came out only at night to feed and left a vicious red bite on the skin of their victims. But I'm not convinced that this was the only reason that kept Mother from allowing me to invite Annie to stay overnight because, as far as I know, the Kachmarskis were as free of bedbugs as we were. I think it was something else.

The teachers and schoolchildren seemed to hold no prejudices toward

50

the immigrant youngsters, but I think our parents did, whether they ever admitted it or not. The West was supposed to be the place where everyone was accepted at face value regardless of creed and nationality, and it may have been better than in other parts of the country, but there was still discrimination even if it didn't have a name put to it. Of course most of the Ukrainian and Polish immigrants were Catholic, so that also separated them from us — they attended different services and were not usually invited to our picnics nor church functions.

In any event, most of those children, having to dig down deeper into their inner reserves, did well for themselves. At the Brock Brick School Reunion, I ran into a svelte, beautifully dressed woman who turned out to be Annie Kachmarski. Her achievements far our-circled mine, so this time it was I who felt inferior. With all her degrees and other accomplishments she was out of my sphere, and I didn't get as much pleasure out of meeting my old dancing partner as I had hoped to.

We were taught to be very patriotic and nationalistic at school. Every morning, we pledged allegiance to the flag and sang "God Save the King." Then, after repeating the Lord's Prayer and doing fifteen minutes of physical jerks (exercises), we were ready to start classes.

In the afternoon we had a session of singing. One of the songs that was most popular and which we belted out with gusto was

> Rule Britannia, Britannia rules the waves.
> Britons never, never, never shall be slaves.

And my heart would almost burst with pride when we sang "The Maple Leaf Forever":

> In days of yore from Britain's shore,
> Wolfe, the dauntless hero came
> And planted firm Britannia's flag
> On Canada's fair domain.
> Here may it wave, our boast and pride,
> And join our hearts together.
> The thistle, shamrock, rose, entwined,
> The maple leaf forever.

Fifty years later in this multicultural country, those songs sound very out of place, and perhaps they were out of place even then, but it was an era when most took allegiance to Country, King, and Empire very seriously indeed.

We sang other songs, of course, and because I loved to sing my voice was often raised high above the rest, once to my great embarrassment. We were singing "My Darling Clementine," and since I was just learning to read, when we came to the part "Herr-ing boxes without topses were the shoes for

51

Clementine" I sang, "Her ring boxes without topses ... " and I have to admit I wondered how in the world Clementine could get her feet into small ring boxes. Well, Hank Groz, who sat in front of me and got the full benefit of my loud voice, started to snicker, flapped his hand to get the teacher's attention, and announced to everyone my silly mistake. Embarrassed almost to tears, I wished I could drop out of sight, and to this day I never hear that old song without squirming a bit.

Another little boy who sat near me in those early school days was Eddie Cyr. He was a quiet little fellow and the only thing that stood out about him, as far as I was concerned, were his small square hands with such blunt fingers they looked as if the ends had been chopped off with a knife. Years later, at a dance at Centralia (Ontario) Airforce Training Station, a handsome young airman came up and asked me to dance. When I tried to make conversation, he remained quiet and aloof until I happened to glance at his hand holding mine. The sight of his square fingers stirred something in my memory, and I looked into a mischievously grinning face and gasped, "Why, you're Eddie Cyr, aren't you?" (He had already recognized me.) Funny what the memory holds.

Mike Sherban was another boy who started school with me. His father was a foreman on the gang that looked after the railroads, and Mike's family lived in a house supplied by the Canadian National Railway right beside the tracks. They had recently emigrated from Eastern Europe and went to the Catholic church, so he was another child I hadn't known before going to school. For some reason or other, Mike was smitten with my charms, and to my horror didn't mind letting everyone know it. Whenever I glanced at him he seemed to be gaping at me, and he always tried to get on the same team at recess time. I may have been secretly flattered but naturally I had to pretend I "hated" him, and went out of my way to shun his advances.

At one Christmas concert there was a small, mysterious package for me under the tree. When I saw the card that said "To Gwyneth from Mike," I tried to sit on it, but I wasn't fast enough for Bubbles' bright eyes. "Open it, open it!" she demanded. Reluctantly I tore off the paper and lifted the lid of the box to find a pair of dangly, bright blue glass earrings. It was an inappropriate gift for a little girl, but I suspect they were the loveliest things Mike could find. And where he got them would always be a mystery; he surely didn't have the money to buy them so maybe he begged them from his mother's jewellery box. Terrified at being the laughingstock of the whole class, I wanted to throw them away, but Mother insisted I do no such thing, and that I thank Mike graciously for his gift. The words stuck in my throat, but somehow I was able to chew them up and finally spit them out.

Later I came to see that it was a special event since Mike's was the very first gift I ever received from a male admirer, and while over the years I've received my share of beautiful presents, I'm sure none of them was ever given with more admiration than Mike's.

I took to school like a duck to water and my vivid imagination was a help to me most of the time. But on one occasion it put such shame on my head that it took years for me to get over it. After a violent lightning, thunder, and hail storm, many of the children had sensational stories to relate. Several had windows broken by hail; the roof of one family's henhouse was blown off, and another boy told a funny story about how his terrified dog had jumped right into bed with him at the height of the storm. Not wanting to be left out, I raised my hand. "Yes, Gwyneth," said the teacher, "What happened at your house?"

To this day I don't understand why, except that I wanted to be in the limelight, but I blurted out, "Our house was struck with lightning!" A gasp went around the room, and Miss Veum's face showed alarm. "Was there much damage?" she asked.

Immediately I knew I was caught in a lie and I wished I'd been hit by that imaginary bolt myself. All eyes were on me, so I had to go on with my story. Stumbling for words, I spluttered out a completely unbelievable tale of how the lightning had struck the outside wall of the livingroom and made a big hole right behind the piano, of how my dad had put out the fire with pails of water and had immediately repaired the wall so that there was now no damage to be seen. The children may have believed my story, but I knew by the look on the face of my beloved Miss Veum that she didn't.

To make matters worse, Bubbles drew me aside at recess. "That was a big lie," she said accusingly, "And I just bet you're going to get a licking."

"You gonna tell?" My eyes implored her not to, but she just tossed her blonde head and ran to play with the other kids. I knew if she did tell her parents it was game over for me because they'd be sure to mention it to my mother and dad.

That night I waited for the boom to lower, but it didn't, and for a week I lived in dread fear they'd find out what a great disappointment I was to them. The shame of it hung over me like a black cloud so that I couldn't sleep or eat, and Mother began to think I was coming down with something. I confessed my sin to God every night and promised Him that if He would only keep this disgrace from my parents I would never, never, never tell another lie in my whole life.

If Bubbles told, or if my Mother and Dad found out, they didn't let on; perhaps they laughed it off as another one of my wild imaginary flights. I never had the courage to ask them. It was never any laughing matter to me. That lie and the humiliation it brought to my inner self haunted me for decades, and whenever I was tempted to embellish a story to make it a little more exciting my throat got as dry as sandpaper.

School work came fairly easy to me so I was allowed to skip Grade 6, something I often regretted later. It was no trouble for me to catch up with the mathematics and most of the other subjects, but one thing I did miss was the good grounding in grammar that came in Grade 6. I never did learn the proper construction of a sentence and have always had to speak and write English by the seat of my skirt.

The move up in grades put me in closer contact with students I hadn't known well before. One of these was Betty Stephen, who came from the south of Brock. She was an only child, a little spoiled but a beautiful, vivacious girl with a near perfect complexion. Her parents were Scottish, and I spent many a weekend enjoying their easy-going hospitality. It seemed that Betty was the only person in the whole district who didn't know she was adopted. My mother warned me severely never to mention the fact to Betty, and I never did. But after I left Saskatchewan and Betty was in her mid-teens she came across her adoption papers and the secret was out. It was too bad her parents hadn't told her because it was a terrible shock to her, one, perhaps, from which she never fully recovered. Betty and I remained good friends until her untimely death from an aneurysm in her late forties.

The year I was ready for high school, our popular principal, George MacArthur, moved back to Ontario, so it was a Mr. Giselle who became my Grade 9 teacher. He was a strange man, quick and nervous, with bad breath and little patience. He and his wife, a small, straight-faced woman, lived at the hotel, and I always felt that their relationship was not a happy one.

That year, Mr. Giselle directed a play for the Christmas concert and picked me for the lead role. The part was of a rather worldly young woman, and since I had nothing to wear for such a sophisticated creature, Mr. Giselle offered to lend me one of his wife's dresses. I'll never forget being almost overcome by the smell of stale perfume and body odour whenever I pulled that dress over my head. Needless to say, it took some of the joy out of my performance.

Nevertheless, Mr. Giselle must have been a good teacher because when I moved to Ontario the next year I had absolutely no trouble keeping up with the classes in much larger high schools. As a matter of fact, I was ahead in most subjects, and I've always been proud and grateful for the years I spent in the Brock Brick School.

~

54

Zella Strutt (right).

Betty Stephen (right).

Bubbles Clendening (left).

CHAPTER TWELVE

Transportation Thrills

I f lack of money accentuated all the problems during the Depression, it also nurtured the spirit of inventiveness: everyone learned to "make do" with what they had. This creative spirit showed up in many areas, and no more so than in the kinds of vehicles that carried us across the dry, dusty roads.

Although gasoline was only a few cents a gallon, many a farmer couldn't afford to run his car. So he pulled out the motor, attached a hitch to the chassis so it could be drawn by horses, and called it a "Bennett Buggy."

R. B. Bennett was Prime Minister of Canada from 1930 to 1935 and because Western farmers perceived him as being completely unsympathetic to their plight he became, rightly or wrongly, the butt of their suffering and their jokes. With biting sarcasm they immortalized him by putting his name on this demeaning mode of transportation — a reminder of how tough things really were.

Another transportation problem in the '30s was getting children to and from the consolidated schools which were effectively working in the West by that time. Because the cost of operating schoolbuses was completely out of reach, we (the students) were usually conveyed in horse-drawn canvas-covered vans. For the sum of $1.50 a day, the driver supplied the horses and the vehicle, a narrow box-like affair with a tiny window up front where the driver sat to guide the horses with reins that passed through a small slot. Next came a coal-burning stove, its tin stack smoking blissfully, if not safely, through the roof. A door at the back let riders in and out, and a dozen or so of us sat on seats on either side with our knees touching, huddling up to the fire to keep warm.

56

Of course, we all carried our lunches, but very few of us had anything as fancy as a regular lunch box. Instead, our plain, white bread sandwiches were packed in old lard or honey pails with pressed-on lids and little wire handles by which we swung them. I could nearly always count on Mother to send a tasty lunch with me, which often included one of her fresh biscuits with honey spread in the middle, and if I was lucky a big fat lemon ammonia cookie with a single raisin on top.

Three quiet and well-mannered children from an English family rode with us and it always seemed to me that one of them had a cold, or was fighting a cold, or was getting over one. Even now, whenever I think of that old school van, my nostrils are filled with the strong, bitter smell of the eucalyptus with which their mother rubbed them soundly, the reek of it almost strangling the rest of us.

Our driver was Manson Strutt, who had come to Saskatchewan from Quebec, but with loyal Irish blood still flowing through his veins. Every March 17 we were the only rig that trotted smartly into the Brock school-yard with our horses' tails and manes resplendently braided with flowing green ribbons. No matter what our nationality, those who drove with Manson on St. Patrick's Day were Irish to the core, and proud of it!

When we were small, we passed the hours in the van by singing or play-ing games like I Spy and Birds in the Bush, but as soon as our hands could hold a deck of cards the older pupils taught us how to play Bridge. Although we had never heard of Charles H. Goren, we were Bridge experts by the time we were eight, although I do admit we made up some of our own rules.

Once the good weather arrived, the van was lifted off sleighs onto wheels that bumped and joggled us along narrow dirt roads. We no longer fought to sit close to the stove but instead pushed and shoved to get a seat by the open back door. When the air became too hot and stuffy, we often jogged along behind, getting in shape for the school's field day.

In the fall, we practised our entries for the the verse and speaking contests as we rode along. These were very competitive events against the neigh-bouring schools, so we spent hours preparing and coaching each other in the hope that our Brock team could take the honours.

Occasionally in winter, we'd hit an unexpectedly hard snowdrift that would tip us over, tumbling children, stove, books, and lunch pails into chaos. This may have been dangerous, but we always considered it an exciting diversion and a great story to relate at school.

We country children always hoped for a blizzard that would make it too hazardous for the van to set out for home. These hopes were usually realized at least once every winter, when we happily watched thick white snow sweep steadily across the flat land to block out all landmarks. Then, filled with anticipation for a night of fun, we would be assigned to the home of a friend who lived in town or be put up at the white frame hotel in the middle of the village. What a lark that was! Bunking three or four to a bed didn't make for sleep, but it certainly produced plenty of highjinks and squealing as the boys peeked over transoms or raced down the dark halls banging on every door. While the wind howled and the snow piled up, Mr. and Mrs. Chant, the poor hotel keepers, spent the whole sleepless night praying fervently for the weather to break.

And it usually did, the next day dawning crystal clear, the brilliant sun and deep blue arch of sky belying the fierce storm of the night before. Fortunately, the teachers didn't expect us to be as bright as the day when we arrived at school dozy and bleary-eyed.

Sometimes the van was used to transport us to a dance in town, with one of the older boys driving the horses. Going there, the time passed quickly as we chattered and joked while the young driver urged the team to a fast trot. But coming home, ah, that was another story. The horses were encouraged to drift along to make the night stretch as long as possible. The pitch blackness always made some of the occupants a little bolder; shocking stories were whispered in the dark while the "fast" ones petted in the corners.

I was about thirteen when I was first allowed out on one of these jaunts, mostly because my brother Art was driving the team and was supposed to look out for me. Coming home, sitting in the quiet dark, I drowsed off and my head fell against the shoulder of a fifteen-year-old boy, Earl Elviss, sitting beside me. Apparently that was all the encouragement Earl needed. Grabbing me and knocking off my round steel-rimmed glasses, he planted a sloppy kiss on my astonished lips.

Although it was my very first kiss from a boy, it certainly was not very romantic, and I remember as I felt around for my glasses I thought disgustedly, "So that's what it's like. Ye gods, it sure ain't what it's cracked up to be!"

Ah yes, we learned a great deal travelling in those hard-time vehicles, much more, I think, than our parents ever dreamed.

~

CHAPTER THIRTEEN

Chicken in the Pot

 hen I was a little girl our fresh meat came right off the hoof, and I learned young that if I was to have a full stomach I couldn't capitulate to squeamishness when it came to killing animals for food. Although there were no supermarkets from which to buy, I knew very well that there was a price to pay for chicken in the pot.

When the men were away, Mother commandeered me to chase a squawking rooster around the barn until we cornered it and got it in our clutches. Then, while the poor bird struggled and frantically flapped its wings, I was somehow expected to hold it firmly by its scaly yellow legs, its terrified head on a block of wood while Mother took deadly aim with the axe.

This was, indeed, a cheerless task, but if we had received a call that the minister or some other visitor was coming for supper, there was no way out. The terror of the squawking bird was second only to my own, and often, just as Mother was bringing down the axe, something compelled me to let go, so that the rooster dashed to ecstatic freedom, to Mother's furious disgust. Of course we had to begin the chase all over, but this time, even though I found the act just as distasteful, I didn't dare rouse Mother's anger further, so when I saw the axe rise high in the air I hung on for dear life. At the sound of the dull, lethal "chop," I let loose the struggling legs to behold the headless chicken raising the dust with its still-flapping wings and circling in a fanatical, jerky dance. "Oh, the poor thing," I'd cry, "It's still alive."

"It is *not* alive!" Mother would exclaim crossly, but I knew she was just as relieved as I was when it finally gave up cavorting that mad dance of death and dropped, giving one last feeble kick.

While I held my breath against the vile acrid smell, we plunged the bird into a kettle of hot water to loosen the feathers so they could be plucked more easily. Repulsed yet fascinated, I helped to pull out the still warm, slimy intestines, the tiny black heart, the gizzard filled with the chicken's last meal of grain and gravel, the delicate pink lungs, and lastly, the rough-ribbed windpipe. It was an early lesson in anatomy that later stood me in good stead in high school zoology. When the bird was thoroughly washed and wiped out, the tiny hairs were singed off its white limp body as we dangled it over a blazing newspaper cone. Then Mother whacked it into pieces and tossed them into the big aluminum pot.

Two hours later, with all our murderous dealings behind us, I licked up my plate of her famous chicken dumpling stew with never a thought for the unfortunate creature that had been unsuspectingly preening its feathers a short time earlier.

Before the invention of household refrigeration, beef rings kept many farmers' families supplied with fresh meat all summer. In the Beef Ring Association to which we belonged, each farmer-member agreed to provide a good steer once during the summer. He paid five dollars to Dad, who supplied the slaughterhouse, butchered the animal, and divided the cuts evenly among the members. To aid him in this he had a large diagram of a side of beef hung on the wall, showing all the various cuts, each one bearing a number. Beside that diagram was another chart listing all the members' names, where Dad carefully marked down the number of cuts that each received.

Thus it was that each week a beef ring member received at least one good cut along with poorer ones until by the end of the summer every family had eaten its way through a whole carcass. It usually turned out that a farmer would receive only one brisket (the poorest cut) and one rump roast (the choicest cut). And although Dad kept meticulous records, he was some-times accused of switching the cuts. There was always a reason for this false accusation. In the dry years of the '30s, a farmer might not own an A-1 steer, so he would bring an old animal instead, or one for which there hadn't been proper food and whose meat would be tough and stringy, making all of the cuts of meat inferior. It was then that someone was bound to accuse Dad of giving him a poor cut when he knew it was his turn to receive a good one. Dad would have to lead him to the charts and patiently explain that the irate member had really received a good cut from a poor animal and not a poor cut from a good beast as he supposed.

In spite of these sometimes annoying tangles, Dad ran the beef ring for as far back as I can remember, starting sometime in the '20s. The building itself stood about a quarter of a mile from the house in the corner of one of our fields. It had a small corral where a steer was unloaded every Friday afternoon.

Right after supper, Art and Carf and I trekked behind Dad as he stalked to the slaughterhouse to commence his grisly business. The boys shooed the animal into a small chute against the building. My sympathies were always with the steer when a rope was placed around its neck and then looped over a board of the chute and held fast so the animal couldn't move its head. This took a fair amount of strength on my brothers' part, because the steer, wild-eyed with panic, had begun by this time to see the writing on the wall.

While the boys held the rope taut, Dad climbed up the side of the chute and, balancing himself precariously, lifted a mammoth sledgehammer high above his head. I shut my eyes and cringed when he brought it down with a mightly crack on the skull of the animal.

The steer fell like a ton of bricks and rolled through a shallow hinged door onto a depression on the cement floor of the slaughterhouse. Immediately its throat was slashed with a long, razor-sharp knife to allow the blood to gurgle outside through a small trench. The blood was caught in pails and some of it carried home to fertilize Mother's houseplants, which, needless to say, grew wild and strong in her sunporch!

Dad, with the help of my brothers, skinned the animal deftly, removed its entrails, and with chain and pulley hoisted it up to hang from a beam overnight. Next morning at the crack of dawn he was rustling the boys out of bed to help with the butchering.

When they grew up and moved away, I was chosen to be his assistant. I never minded. I loved working with my kind, gentle father, and although somewhat squeamish about the actual killing, was rather fascinated by the rest of the procedure.

While he sawed and cut up the carcass, my job was to mark the charts and see that everyone got the proper pieces of meat, which I placed in bleached sugar bags. Each family had its name embroidered on its bag, and some of the labels were quite fancy, depending on the artistic ability of the woman of the house. By noon, all the white bags filled with fresh meat had been picked up and the slaughterhouse floor scrubbed clean.

The heart, liver, and hide (which might bring a dollar or so) were the property of the family that supplied the animal. Because the liver was so large, most farmers were glad to share a few slices with us. Therefore, our Saturday noontime meal, every summer, was fried liver smothered in onions and rich, thick gravy. I can taste it yet, and have never found anything as delectable in any fancy restaurant anywhere.

Roasts were large and cooked slowly in the kitchen's coal range oven. We ate off one for days, first hot, then cold thick slices with Mother's homebaked white bread and green tomato relish. Finally the remainder was minced in the meat grinder for a succulent Shepherd's Pie fit for the gods.

To add pork to our diet, we killed a pig in the early winter. This was quite a different operation from the beef ring because the hog was slaughtered right in our own snowy yard. After the squealing pig had been "stuck," its carcass was hung on a tripod to be disembowelled and then dipped into a huge tub of scalding water to make it easier to scrape the hair off its hide.

It was a busy, bustling time for everyone. The fat was brought into the house for Mother to render into baking lard in the oven, and we children thought the residue of crunchy brown crackles, which melted in our mouths, as good as any candy. The feet and head were boiled in a big cooper kettle until the meat fell off the bones. The meat was then made into jellied headcheese, pressed into brown crocks, and stored in the cool basement. The hams were cured in a saltpetre and placed in deep barrels.

The day we killed the hog was one of excitement, especially for Carf and Art. They stood around waiting for Dad to remove and carefully empty the pig's bladder. Then, inserting a grain straw into the small opening, they puffed out their cheeks and blew up the bladder, turning it into a tough, lopsided ball. After tying it with a bit of cord, one of them would give it a mighty kick, and a raucous game of football followed, lasting just as long as the pig's tough bladder!

In those days, we didn't waste a thing, and even the youngest of us accepted the law of nature that sacrifice was often the way to our survival. We knew exactly where our food came from and the process of getting it to our table.

~

Chapter Fourteen

Brock, Sask.

The Canadian National Railway, pushing through from Rosetown toward Kindersley in the fall of 1909, passed through the Brock site on the edge of virgin prairie that swept north, east, and west as far as the eye could scan. To the south, a low ridge of coulee hills rippled through the otherwise flat and untreed land. Some settlers had taken up land in the area a few years earlier, coming in over a hundred miles by ox cart or on horse-drawn wagons and living in sod huts. However, the summer after the railway arrived, Brock was just a scrabbly tent town with the intrepid pioneers living and conducting business under canvas or in makeshift shacks until permanent buildings could be erected.

As more and more settlers arrived, businesses sprang up, and by 1913 when my parents landed in Brock, the town was mushrooming. The first of four towering grain elevators, landmarks of the prairies, was built in 1910. That same year, an impressive three-storey hotel, the Metropole, was erected to accommodate people flocking in to buy land. It was at this hotel that my grandparents stayed in 1912 when they were on a trip through the West, and it was here that Grandfather Cann happened to overhear some land speculators from the United States discussing the purchase of land in the Brock district. Convinced that they were on to a good thing, Grandfather followed suit and went out next morning to buy a section of unbroken land about three miles northeast of town. Persuaded that he was purchasing an unprecedented opportunity for his family, he immediately set out for Regina to persuade his son, Lawrence, who was working there, to give up his job and move to Brock. Then he and Grandmother returned to Ontario

The Metropole Hotel, built in 1910 to accommodate the settlers coming in to take up land around Brock. Note the formal dress of the people.

to buy up the necessary machinery and horses, pick up their teenage son, Art, and persuade my mother and father to join them in the glorious adventure of farming in Saskatchewan.

Of course Brock, with its hundred or so residents, was no longer booming in the 1930s, but was still an important centre for all the farmers in the area. It had two general stores, two hardwares, a drug store, butcher shop, Chinese restaurant, post office, lumber yard, bank, pool hall, munici-pal office, a rink, the hotel, two churches, the railway station, barber shop, and grain elevators. The main street ran north and south horizontal to the railway tracks, the station at one end and the white brick school at the other. Most of the businesses, with their high, false fronts, were strung along on either side of the block nearest the station and separated by a dusty dirt road with a well-worn board sidewalk along the front of the buildings. It was a typical, run-down prairie hamlet of the Depression, but it still met most of our needs. Only rarely did we travel to the larger centres of Kindersley or Rosetown, and still more rarely to Saskatoon, one hundred miles away.

To the south of Brock was the coulee, and a little to the east a wide ex-panse of municipal pasture, and both of these spots fascinated me as a child. Although I often drove through the coulee with my family to visit our friends, the Sib Irwins near Eston, it was a rare and blessed occasion when I was allowed to roam around on foot.

The coulee was hauntingly beautiful to me: a series of low hills and gullies rolling gently off to the east and west, barren of foliage except for prairie grass, which during the drought was brittle and gray as it struggled in the land which cracked open for want of rain. No cultivator had torn up

The Brock CNR station. Station agent Fred Groz lived there with his family. We all gathered at the station on Saturday nights to watch the train come in.

its crown, and it was still as wild and free as it had ever been, whispering to me of the not so distant past before the white man arrived with his brawn, his plows, and his railways to conquer the quiet land where the Indians had wandered.

In later years when I visited Brock, I drove to the highest point of the road that cuts through the coulee and saw the land spread out before me for miles and miles on every side like a huge velvet quilt intricately patterned with green crops and brown summer-fallowed fields stitched by narrow black roads and scattered with granaries and other farm buildings. At my feet the tiny village of Brock still huddled against the railway tracks. It was a breathtaking view, one of the most splendid and prosperous I've ever seen. The coulee hills where I stood were still as untamed and primitive, I realized, as they had been *millions* of years ago, but aroused the same deep, wondrous feelings within me as they had when I was a child.

In the summertime, Dad kept his cattle, as did many farmers, in the municipal pasture east of Brock. Unlike the rolling coulee, the pasture was completely flat and ridden with rocks. What intrigued me were the humps of ground one found every so often and the deep wallows where, Dad told me, the buffalo had rolled in the days when great herds of them roamed the land. While he checked on the cattle and put out salt blocks for them, I sat on a big black rock and dreamed about the long-gone buffalo and the strange rounded hummock nearby, which I supposed to be an ancient burial ground. I closed my eyes and immediately saw a tribe of Indians dressed in leather and bright feathers pass by silently, and a small black-haired girl my age beckoned for me to follow. Then Dad called, and I opened my eyes to the

65

empty prairie, jumped up, and ran to the little truck where he was waiting patiently.

The social event of the week in the summer was to go to town on Saturday night. Dressed up in our best, we were joined by everyone for miles around, their cars or horse-drawn vehicles crowding the tiny business section. When our mothers had money they shopped for a few supplies, but mostly they just sat in each other's cars, visiting and catching up on all the community news. Meanwhile, the men stood in small knots leaning on the store-fronts, conversing deeply about crops, the price of wheat, the state of the country, and the "abominable" government in Ottawa. We little girls, our arms entwined around each other's necks, promenaded round and round the board sidewalk, whispering secrets and giggling and trying to ignore the boisterous boys who darted out from behind dark buildings playing tag or trying to slip into the pool hall without their mothers noticing.

It was during this period that Ted Gandy, one of the hardware men, rigged up a small power plant so that the merchants and some of the residents had electric lights from dusk to bedtime (I think Ted decided when it was bed-time!). Electric lights made coming to town even more exciting, because now we were thoroughly modern!

Sometimes we had a penny or two to spend on candy, and once in a while even a nickel (though not as a general rule). One Saturday night I approached Dad, who was talking to some of his friends, and asked him for a nickel. He turned me down quite gruffly and rather hurt my feelings. The next day, he took me aside and gently told me I was never to ask him for money in front of his friends again. Although he didn't say so in so many words, I knew I had embarrassed him by asking for a nickel when he didn't have even a cent in his pocket.

The highlight of Saturday night was the arrival of the western-bound CNR train. Coming from Saskatoon, it passed through Brock at 9:15, and everybody in town crowded on the wooden station platform to meet it. My heart pounded with excitement, and I don't think anything has ever matched the thrill I felt at the sight of that on-coming train. First there was the distant, wavering call, Oooo-oo-Oooo, and then the headlight coming around the bend, almost blinding us with its glaring, searching eye. With a great show of puffing and hissing, white clouds of steam threw up bits of rough cinders into our blinking eyes, while the long black train slid to a magnificent screeching halt. Mailbags were flung out to waiting wagons, as were boxes of drygoods and groceries and sometimes long stems of yellow bananas and crates of oranges for the stores.

The event that caused the greatest excitement was the disembarkation of

Brock much as I remember it as a child, looking to the northwest.

passengers. The air was electric as we all pressed around the exit of a Pullman car where a blue-suited, red-capped conductor smartly set down his small iron stool. After such expectation, if no one stepped down we felt positively cheated, but usually we weren't disappointed. There might be a local businessman returning from a trip to the city, or occasionally, and better still, a mysterious stranger involved in who knew what kind of intrigue!

No matter who detrained, no royal party ever received a more curious or appreciative reception. Four years after I left Brock I went back for my first visit and purposely arrived on the Saturday night train just to enjoy that marvellous heady welcome, which made me feel like a movie star.

After stopping for only a few moments, the locomotive puffed up steam again and pulled from the station. As it rolled by us, we caught glimpses of passengers eating at small tables in the dining car, or a white-coated black porter making up berths for those travelling on to Calgary or other distant places. Our hearts overflowed with envy, and we dreamed of the time when we would not just stand and watch the train pass from view, but would be one of those passengers travelling to far and fascinating fields of adventure.

As the great, lumbering train snaked its way into the darkness and its last lonely wail died on the night, we turned our backs on our dreams, walked down the wooden steps to the dirt road below, hunted up our families, and headed back to the reality of our Depression farm homes.

~

CHAPTER FIFTEEN

Gentle Friends, Invincible Neighbours

ur neighbours, Manson and Violet Strutt, Joe and Laura Salkeld, and Earl and Isabelle Clendening, were as dear to me as aunts and uncles. None of them had much to share in the way of this world's goods, but what they gave me in love and personal interest was much more important.

For the most part, all of our homes were plain and simple, with none of today's opulent furnishings and appliances. Many of our neighbours still lived in the small gray houses that they had first put up on the prairie, hoping there would soon be money to build a bigger and better one. The Depression killed those dreams, but despite their humble appearances, those houses radiated the kind of warm welcome that could not be surpassed in a millionaire's castle.

The brown cedar-shingled house Mother and Dad built in 1918 was never really completed. The original plan called for two more rooms to be added on at a future date, but this never happened. Hence what was to be the kitchen became the diningroom, and the original diningroom became the livingroom. A deserted two-room pioneer shack was drawn up alongside the house for a kitchen and a bedroom which the boys used only in the good weather. Off the dining and living rooms was a large vestibule with a dark stained staircase going to the second floor where there were two bedrooms and an unfinished bathroom. This little room under the slanting eaves was barely large enough to hold a steel pull-out couch on which Carf and Art slept during the winter. Our "facilities" were primitive, a two-holer out behind the granary in the yard in the summer or a covered granite pail in the clothes closet in the winter. We did our morning washing up at the dry sink in the corner of the kitchen where there was a hand pump to bring water from the cistern (when it wasn't dry) and a pail underneath to catch the slops. Our weekly baths took place in a tub in front of the kitchen's big black range, which served as a cookstove and heater.

There was no hydro, of course; our main illumination came from kerosene lamps whose soft flickering light never reached the corners of the room. In the evening, one was placed in the centre of the diningroom table and we all sat round sharing its yellow glow, Dad scanning the *Saskatoon Star Phoenix*, Mother mending socks or overalls, and we children working at our homework or playing a game of cards. Although both Mother and Dad were brought up believing that only the wicked played cards — Mother often related how her own mother threw all the decks of cards she found in her sons' pockets into the fire — and although neither of them enjoyed playing cards, they had broadened their views to believe that it was a harmless pastime for their offspring. So we played often in the glow of the lamp.

If the wick became uneven, the light wouldn't be as bright and would make the flame smoke, blackening the glass chimney. When I got to be old enough, it was one of my Saturday morning duties to trim the wicks and polish the chimneys, not something I particularly enjoyed.

Little silk mantles replaced the wicks when gasoline lamps and lanterns were introduced. When lit, they became incandescent, throwing out a bright white light, and although they certainly pushed back the shadows much farther, their light always seemed harsh and stark compared to the friendly golden gleam of the coal-oil lamps.

One utility we did have was the telephone. It came into the area around 1917, and Dad was one of the men who strung up the first lines. Ours hung on the wall of the diningroom, a brown oak box with the black mouthpiece sticking out in front while the receiver was hooked on the side. We shared the line with many other subscribers, so it was often busy. One long ring and two short ones meant someone was calling us, and if we wanted to speak to someone on another line we gave "central" one long ring and asked her to connect us. The central office was housed in the MacLeod home in Brock, where family members acted as the operators.

It's difficult to imagine how we could have managed without the telephone — so many people lived long distances from town and from their neighbours. Although we were fortunate to have other families living

Dad took a course on repairing telephone lines (Regina, 1917).

69

fairly close, others were in more isolated areas, with the telephone their one link to the rest of the community. Many a night we were awakened by the incessant jangling of the telephone calling Mother and Dad to someone's assistance. It might be that a sick child needed to be taken to the doctor or, as I remember on two occasions, that a family needed comfort and help when someone died suddenly.

Because our kitchen lean-to was just a shell of a place, it was almost impossible to heat in winter, so Mother got the idea of moving the kitchen to the basement in the cold weather. It was anything but beautiful with its rough cement walls and floors and the small high windows that let in very little light. In one corner under the stairs was a square cement cistern to catch the precious rainfall; in another was a large coal bin with our supply of winter fuel; and in another a smaller bin holding our potatoes and whatever vegetables we might have been able to grow. In the centre of the floor stood a great furnace that consumed tons of coal and had to be stoked constantly to be convinced to give heat to the upper rooms. So it was in the limited space left over from the cistern, the furnace, and the coal and potato bins that Mother set up her winter kitchen.

To brighten it up she gave the walls a coat of whitewash and spread an old piece of linoleum on the floor. There was a minimum of furniture: an old range for cooking, a long table covered with blue and white oilcloth, a few straight-backed chairs, a cupboard for holding dishes, pots and pans, and of course Mother's rocking chair pulled up beside the stove. But it was warm and cozy, and I was happy to move into the basement when the cold winds began to blow in snow from the north.

After five long months, however, we were even happier when Mother announced it was time to move back to the summer kitchen. It meant spring had finally arrived, and like gophers we came out of our hole in the ground, dragging Mother's rocking chair with us.

This was the time she started her yearly housecleaning, leaving not a speck of dirt anywhere. Dad was commandeered to haul out all the mattresses and beat them to a pulp while she wiped every coiled bedspring with a damp cloth. Blankets and mats were hung out to blow on the clothesline, and lace curtains were hand-washed, strung on wooden stretchers, and not put up again until every window was shining. Wallpaper was too expensive, but if there were a few cents for a pail of calcimine the walls were freshened up in colours of pale blue, pink, or beige. Sometimes linoleum was painted to cover the worn spots and given a mottled pattern by dipping a sponge or even a cut potato into another colour and applying it on the first coat. And although we couldn't afford furniture polish, Mother made up a mixture of coal oil and turpentine which, when rubbed on the diningroom suite, gave it a lustre in which you could see your face. Although our house had no fancy furniture, it was certainly clean. Mother made it cheerful too with her colourful hooked rugs, brightly embroidered cushions, healthy green plants, and sometimes a bowl of highly polished red apples in the middle of the table.

Every Saturday morning the whole house had to be mopped and dusted from top to bottom. In the livingroom there was an elephant hide and wicker set consisting of a settee and two large chairs. It was quite elegant with its dark brown leather and deeply rolled wicker arms and trim. Mother and Dad bought it second-hand from Louis Keil, the hardware merchant, when he and his family moved to Vancouver. It was the first good furniture we ever owned and cost next to nothing. Mother was extremely proud of it, and about twice a month it had to be cleaned and buffed with brown shoe polish.

The Clendenings had the newest and best house in our area. It was built about 1928, just before the Depression, and was the first and only house around to have a real working bathroom complete with septic toilet. The big white cast-iron tub was a novelty too, and what fun Bubbles, June, and I had sliding around in it, splashing water until the floor was awash and their mother came running up the stairs to make us wipe it up.

Mrs. Clendening was an Irish lady who loved to sing and dance. She taught us three girls the Highland Fling and the Irish Jig while she pounded

out the tunes on the piano. When Bubbles and I were about eight and June six, Mrs. Clendening and Mother made us Scottish outfits, and we danced our way to second place at an amateur contest in D'arcy, a small town east of Brock, while our fathers beamed and applauded proudly.

Earl Clendening was a wonderful man, a whimsical wag who playfully teased us. He was one of the first to take up a homestead in the area in 1906, several years before the railway line came through, and his story itself would fill a book. He loved his children with a passion, and was always warmhearted to me too.

Wedding picture of our good neighbours, Isabelle and Earl Clendening.

He and Dad and all the other men

71

called each other by their first names, but Mother and her friends, although they used to say they were "closer than sisters," always addressed each other formally as Mrs. Clendening, Mrs. Strutt, Mrs. Salkeld, and Mrs. Cann. And woe betide any of us children if we ever made the fatal mistake of calling an elder by his or her first name. Such disrespect would have been a punishable offence.

While the Clendenings lived a mile to the east, Laura and Joe Salkeld lived a mile to the west in a tiny gray house. Joe was a bright-faced Englishman whose clear blue eyes smiled out behind round glasses. He never completely lost his accent, and we always tittered

The Salkeld family: Bob, Hudson, Laura, Evelyn, and Joe, taken in the 1940s.

when he called Carf and Art "Caf and At." Laura was a pretty dark-haired young woman whom Joe had met in Manitoba, where he had stopped for a time before settling near Brock.

They had a son, Bob, a year or two younger than I, and a little girl, Evelyn, two years younger than he. Once they were sent to spend the night with us while their mother was having a baby at home (where we were all born in those days). The next morning, the telephone call came with the news that they had a baby brother, but Bob would have none of it. No matter how Mother tried to convince him, he wouldn't believe it. He and I went off to school in the van, and in the late afternoon when he was being dropped off at his gate he was still insisting, "I don't have no baby brother!" He did venture so far as to say that there "might" be a new baby calf at the barn. When he jumped out of the van to high-tail it to the house and found that the news was really true, however, he was delighted.

From an early age Bob had the most terrible yen to fly. On the rare occasion when a small plane passed overhead he'd be beside himself, galloping after the plane looking skyward, running into fences and falling over himself, all the while crying and begging the unsuspecting pilot, "Please, please, come and take me!"

He was positive that he and I could fly if we just had enough faith. His faith was stronger than mine, and many's the time he pushed me off the peak of the barn roof after tying a couple of tea towels to my arms, shouting "Flap harder, flap harder!" Fortunately, there was always a soft pile of straw below. When World War II broke out, he surprised everyone by joining the navy instead of the airforce.

Evelyn was a replica of her mother. She spent a good deal of time at our place, once for several weeks while her mother went back to her home in Manitoba because of an illness in the family. Evelyn always called my mother "Mrs. Alex" and went around chattering from dawn to dusk. Sometimes when she tagged along after Carf and Art they'd get tired of her constant babbling and say, "Oh, go tell Mother she wants you." And she'd trot off to find Mother, lisping innocently, "You want me, Mrs. Alex!"

Hudson, Bob and Evelyn's baby brother, was named after an uncle who was an officer in the Royal Canadian Mounted Police in the far north. He was the first baby I'd ever had much to do with, and I adored him so much that I prayed Mother and Dad would have a baby just like him. That was one prayer Mother had no intention of answering, although she too was smitten with Hudson's charms and loved to cuddle him in her rocking chair.

It's impossible to think about my childhood without remembering the Strutt family that lived about a mile and a quarter to the north. Like many others, Manson and his auburn-haired wife, Violet, came to Saskatchewan from Ontario, somewhere near Ottawa. They had three children older than I, Elva around Art's age, Zella a year or so younger, and Herb a couple of years younger yet. Then came Glenn, who was born after me, and finally, blue-eyed Gwennie May, who brought up the rear several years later.

Up to their necks in the oats are my father and Manson Strutt holding Herb Strutt on their shoulders. With me (left) are Zella and Elva Strutt. Two days later the crop was flattened by wind and most of it lost.

73

When the older kids were off to school, Glen would accompany his mother when she came to help my mother with a quilt, and although he was the cutest curly-haired little fellow you ever saw, he was like a demon possessed when he swung my precious cats around by their tails. I'd fly into him with both fists flashing until his mother or mine crossly pulled us apart. Although Herb was younger than my brothers, he was their great friend, and when he joined forces with them to tease me he was not my favorite visitor. Nevertheless, there was a deep bond between all us Canns and Strutts, with much going back and forth to each other's house.

They had a gramophone, and we kids loved to crank it up by the handle on the side and listen to the lively tunes of "Turkey in the Straw" or "Sipping Cider Through a Straw," a song never heard before or since but which always got my toes tapping. Sometimes I stayed overnight, snuggling down between Elva and Zella, both of whom I loved, and we whispered long into the night. The girls' bedroom was off the kitchen and I always remember waking up in the morning to the smell of toast as Mrs. Strutt held bread in a flat wire basket over the hot range.

Zella had beautiful thick hair, soft brown and wavy. In comparison, mine was cut in a short buster brown style with bangs, and straight as a board. When we were about twelve and ten, she sometimes took pity on me and tried to put some waves in mine. First she boiled up flaxseed until the liquid was a thick slimy mass. Using this as wave setter, she combed it into my short hair, pushing it into waves held in place by black bobby pins until it dried as hard as a rock. The fact that it left my hair feeling and looking like picture wire was of no consequence as long as it had some kink!

The Strutt family presented a lesson in patience and love. Elva, their first child, was born handicapped, her right side deformed so that she dragged her leg and had little use of her right hand. And though she tried her mightiest to speak, her speech was indecipherable to nearly everyone but her family. Despite her handicaps, Elva was a lovely, sensitive youngster with a great capacity to love who could see a joke quicker than most of us.

This was long before there were assocations for the physically or mentally handicapped to give support to parents, and there were no group homes as there are today. It was a difficult, heartbreaking situation, but Elva's parents coped with great strength and wisdom. While she was never babied, and was treated the same as other members of the family, her sisters and brothers knew there were times when she did need their special attention and help, and they gave it to her cheerfully, as a matter of course, with no complaints. She was never looked down upon and was made to feel as important as anyone and worthy of her place in the world.

Special neighbours, the Strutt family: (back) Zella, Elva, Herb, Glen; (front) Violet, Gwennie May, and Manson (taken in the 1940s).

She road the van to school with the rest of us, struggling to make her letters with her left hand and taking part in all our games. When we played ball, the pitcher made sure to hit her bat, and the catcher always seemed to drop the ball when she came limping for home, the rest of us cheering her on.

Because she was such an affectionate girl herself, and because her family showed great love for her, the rest of us loved her too. By the Strutts' example, we learned that no matter how handicapped a person is, she or he is worthy of our respect and admiration.

There was love, too, in the home of Ethel and Clarence Stankie, a young couple who lived less than a quarter of a mile away. In that smallest of houses, really only two rooms, they produced a beautiful baby every year or so until there were five girls and one boy. Although the house was bursting at the seams and cluttered with children, it was still large enough to hold Ethel's robust laughter and Clarence's gentle, patient optimism.

Clarence, ten years older than Ethel, came from Ontario with his family, and was in rather delicate health when he fell in love with the vivacious dark beauty who was supposed to marry his younger brother. Ethel, realizing he was far the better of the two, accepted his proposal and moved with him to California, where the doctors thought his health would improve. This didn't happen, but when they returned to Saskatchewan to visit Ethel's family and he began to feel better, they decided to move back for good. Unfortunately, it was just when the Depression struck, and times were very hard for them as they tried to scrape out a living from a small, unproductive farm.

Tough as it was, their tiny place was a haven of love. Although I knew my mother and father loved each other, Mother thought any display of affection unseemly, especially in front of the children. With Clarence and Ethel it was different. The love they felt for each other was there for everyone to see, in a pat, a hug, or a kiss on the back of the neck. They were completely different in their personalities; Clarence was quiet and reserved, but when his smiling eyes looked at Ethel they overflowed with tenderness though she might be boisterously boiling over about some matter or another.

She ruled their little nest with a commanding voice, her language laced with the odd colourful blasphemy, merry laughter, and a heavy dose of love. Although not above using some oaths when she wanted to get a point across, she never allowed her children to swear. One day four-year-old Jewel said to three-year-old Clarice, "Say a bad word, Clarice."

Clarice complied. "Damn it to Hell!"

"Clarice Stankie," shrieked her mother, "Don't you dare talk like that!"

Clarice whimpered, "Jewelie told me."

Ethel's wrath turned on little Jewelie, "Jewel! I'm going to spank you!"

Jewel burst into tears. "But I thought she was only going to say Caesar's Ghost!" Ethel's laughter peeled forth and the spanking was forgotten.

Over the years, the slim little girl Clarence had married had put on weight and grown into a hearty, good-looking woman. And each year her tender heart seemed to get bigger, enfolding all who came within her doors. Despite the fact that she was surrounded by her own small children and busy meeting their many needs, she always found sympathy and time for me when I went skipping across the stubbled field for cheering up.

Clarence's health did improve and he lived to be over ninety, still as deeply in love with Ethel as on the day they had met.

When out West a couple of years ago, I visited Ethel, and was amazed when she informed me that the original "Cann shack" had been drawn up on her and Clarence's property years before. "I couldn't see it destroyed," she told me, "Not when it held so many memories."

The five Stankie children: Jewel, Clarice, Johnny, Betty, and Sophia. Eula was yet to be born.

I walked out to the back of the lot and, sure enough, there it stood, an ancient gray wooden shack leaning askew, many boards and shingles missing and the two small windows boarded up. The tarpaper that had once covered it had long since disappeared. I shoved the door open. It scraped noisily along the rough floor where a few kernels of wheat lay in the corners, showing it had once been used as a granary. But there was nothing else, just the sagging shell precariously held together by splintering two by fours. There were no sugar bags pasted on the walls to keep out the cold, there was no aroma of bread baking, no creaking chair rocking two babies to sleep, no laughter, no homesickness, and no tears except those that welled up in my own eyes as I pulled shut the rotting door and walked back to Ethel, the old-time friend who had known me since the day I was born.

Ernie and Viola Hyde lived across the road from the Strutts, and were just like an aunt and uncle to the Strutt children. They were a rare breed, and although they had no children of their own they loved everyone else's and had the knack of making each small person feel very special. They invited one child at a time and gave him or her all their attention. What a treat it was when I was the one asked to spend the night in their small, clean-as-a-whistle house. Viola made fancy food I didn't get at home, dainty triangular sandwiches with the crusts cut off, whipped lemon pudding served in thin glass sherbert dishes, cookies cut out like stars with little silver balls of sugar on top. And her Divinity Fudge and red and green Turkish Delight rolled in icing sugar simply melted in my mouth. We ate off her best blue and white china, a freshly ironed starched white cloth on the table, drank our tea from pretty flowered cups, and wiped our mouths with linen napkins.

After supper, the crokinole board came out, and if I happened to get a checker or two in scoring position Ernie always seemed to miss them or hit the pegs (no matter how hard he tried), declaring that I was the best crokinole player he'd ever come up against. When it was time for bed, Viola tucked me in on a couch in the small bright sun porch between sweet-smelling white sheets beautifully embroidered with her fancy work, my head on a matching pillow slip. Then

All the children in the area loved Viola and Ernie Hyde. Above, Viola holds Glen Strutt, the neighbours' baby.

she read from her big Bible storybook until I fell blissfully asleep. When I left for home the next day, I knew what it was to be royalty.

I knew quite a bit about royalty, especially the little princesses, Elizabeth and Margaret Rose, from listening to Grandma Deakin, who had come from England to live on her son's farm about ten miles away. A bright-faced, roly-poly little lady, she had the clear pink complexion that so many of the English have, and because she looked exactly like what I thought a grandmother should, I called her Grandma Deakin.

Although her relatives were more than kind, she missed her friends and pleasant homeland. Mother, who liked her immensely, invited her to spend part of the winter with us to help with the sewing and, mostly, just to give her a change. I loved Grandma Deakin. She was sweet and kind, telling me stories and showing me her scrapbook filled with pictures of England and the little princesses, whom she adored. She slept with me, wearing her voluminous heavy flannel nightgown, a frilled nightcap, and white woolen socks. And although she smelled strongly of camphorated salve, I was happy to curl up to her broad back on a cold night.

One bitterly stormy night there came a great banging on our door. It was a young lad, Gordon Ham, who lived with his family several miles north of us. He had met his mother with a horse and cutter at the train in Brock, on which she was returning from Saskatoon with a baby whose mother had just died. They were caught in the fierce blizzard, and having made it to our place decided to come in for refuge rather than try to reach home. It took a great deal of banging to waken Dad, and when he did get to the door and see the plight of Mrs. Ham with the tiny baby he ran to the bottom of the stairs and called loudly for Mother to come down.

Grandma Deakin, awakened by all the ruckus, thought the house was on fire, so she jumped out of bed, collected all her precious possessions in the dark, and threw them into her two carpet bags. Then, flying down the stairs, her huge nightgown billowing out like a sail behind her, she kept shouting in her very proper English voice, "What's wrong, Alex? What's wrong, Alex?" Dad was able to placate her and send her back to bed, but Mother could do nothing but double up with laughter at the strange sight of Mrs. Deakin's wild flight down the stairs.

Poor Grandma Deakin. Often homesick for the green hills of England, she finally decided to return to her native Herefordshire in 1934. Once there, she immediately began to long for her good friends back in Saskatchewan, and in less than a year she contracted cancer. Her letters came frequently; one to me (which I still have), dated October, 1938, was full of inquiries about all the neighbours, young and old, and she told me she had the *Saskatoon Star Phoenix* mailed to her to keep her abreast of what was going on in the province. She described in detail her 145-mile trip to London for medical treatments and told how the trains were packed with women and children, each carrying a gas mask, being evacuated to the country to escape the air raids everyone feared were coming.

Another yellowed letter from Mrs. Deakin was written to Mother in December, 1939. The war was on, and although Mrs. Deakin knew she was dying from cancer, she was full of pluck. Her only regret was that she had left Canada. "I wish I was back at your place," she wrote my mother. "You are such great company one could never be lonesome where you are. You never made me feel old. And how is Alex? I wonder if he wants his old overalls mended? I am the one to do that ... if only I was there." Shortly after, we heard she had died.

There was another family, the Will Jicklings, who lived quite a few miles farther north but with whom we visited regularly. Jessie Jickling came from Stratford, Ontario, a petite, bouncy city girl who fell madly in love with the tall dark Will and left the comforts of home and family to

1916: Perky Jessie Jickling on the horse that she drove eight miles to town every Saturday in summer. Behind her is the home filled with the lovely things Jessie brought from Ontario as a bride.

farm in Saskatchewan. The lovely furniture, rugs, oil paintings, and china she brought with her made her home what Mother called "a little palace."

Soft-spoken and slow-moving, Will was a six-foot tall, quiet man with pools of quiet humour shining in his brown eyes. Jessie, on the other hand, was a chirpy little thing who moved like a flash of lightning and whose blue eyes under swept-up auburn hair crinkled with gay laughter.

They had one daughter, Catherine, and although she was older than I, I adored going to the Jicklings for a week for what I always called my "summer holidays." Catherine had beautiful dolls and we played house by the hour, or swung lazily in the white-slatted wooden swing, or dressed up in her mother's old clothes. A snapshot taken when I was twelve shows me wearing her mother's beautiful heavy satin wedding dress — with a waist of sixteen inches.

Jessie Jickling owned some lovely rings which had been handed down to her from her family. One day those rings went missing, throwing Jessie into a panic. Although she was sure she had left them on her dressing table, she, Catherine, and Will made a frantic and thorough search in the house. When the rings failed to appear, she phoned her plight to Mother and Dad, and since there was a possibility that someone had stolen them, they decided to call in the Royal Canadian Mounted Police from Kindersley.

Make-believe: Catherine Jickling in her father's suit, and me in her mother's wedding dress — in 1936, shortly before the sudden death of Catherine's father.

They arrived resplendent in their red jackets and yellow-stripped jodphurs, full of questions: "How long had the rings been missing?" "Had they had any strangers or visitors in the house lately?" In answer to the last query, the Jicklings admitted that, yes, they had entertained friends from Brock on Sunday, having inviting them and their two daughters to dinner. The police pounced on the information: "How old were the daughters?" "What were their occupations?" When told that one of the girls was a nurse in Saskatoon, they were sure she was the culprit because, in those days, some nurses had the reputation of being fast-living women who would resort to anything! The Jicklings protested that they couldn't believe their friends' daughter was a thief, but the police were adamant about questioning her.

What a shock it was to the young girl and her parents when the Mounties arrived at their door with all their interrogations. Although she hotly denied the accusations and her parents were more than indignant, the police still

80

insisted to the distraught Jicklings that she was likely the guilty party. Since there was no evidence, no charges were laid, but the anger of the young woman's family smoldered over the false accusations.

Two weeks later, when Jessie was taking a jacket out of her clothes closet, she found the missing rings pinned to one of her dresses, and she suddenly remembered that she had hurriedly placed them there herself one day when she was leaving the house.

Sick to her soul, she flew to the phone and apologized profusely to the mother of the girl involved, but unfortunately the incident caused a rift between the families that was never completely mended.

Mr. Jickling always said a short grace before meals, but because he spoke so softly many people missed it. If you visited as often as I did, you simply bowed your head, counted to ten fast, and knew it was over. One day, George Krepps called on some business matter — insurance, I think — and was invited to stay for dinner. When Will mumbled his short, low grace, Mr. Krepps misunderstood and took it as an invitation for him to say it. Being a very religious man, he bowed his head and prayed with a great deal of zeal for a good five minutes. Catherine, giggling, kicked me under the table while her mother tried vainly to restrain her own laughter. Taken aback, Will waited politely, though somewhat impatiently, for Mr. Krepps to finish so that they could get on with dinner.

For some reason, the Jicklings didn't own a car. I think Will just didn't trust them. But they did have a fast-stepping chestnut horse that pulled a black high-wheeled buggy and carried Mrs. Jickling and Catherine the eight or nine miles to town every Saturday. It was Catherine's custom to phone me just before they started out, and I stood in an upstairs window straining my eyes until they appeared as a tiny speck coming down a distant little hill. Then I started off as fast as I could, huffing and puffing by the time we met on the road. Catherine would pull me up beside them and we trotted merrily along, chattering like magpies. Stopping at our farm for a brief visit with Mother and a cup of tea, they carried on to Brock, and if I was lucky Mother let me go too. Riding along in that old buggy behind that little horse is one of my happiest memories.

There are other good memories too, of many people we didn't see as often but who still made life richer by their friendships — families such as the Gordon Elvisses, the Sib Irwins, the John Jicklings, the Norman Lambs, and the Louis Keils, to name only a few. While it is true that in many ways it was a hard time in which to grow up, the constant support and love of those stalwart friends and gentle people made it good beyond measure.

~

Chapter Sixteen

Holidays

e didn't take many holidays when I was a youngster. Most summers were hot and dry, and the only place we had to cool off in was the Strutts' dig-out, a small watering hole we shared with the cattle! It was often so muddy that we could almost walk on it, and the drier the weather, the thicker it became! By the end of the summer it was usually little more than a small slimy puddle. Still, we had plenty of fun there, and I remember sitting and watching the lovely bright darning needles dart and swoop among the weeds growing around the edges.

Before the Depression, when I was about four or five, Dad's uncle and aunt, Alex and Pearl Jamieson from Ontario, drove West in a touring car. They stopped at our farm for a week or so and then persuaded Dad and Mother to accompany them to Chilliwack to visit Grandpa and Grandma Cann (Alex Jamieson was Grandma's brother). Dad decided that the boys and Lola were old enough to look after the place, so off we went.

The only consideration was that we had to be back in time for Lola to leave on holidays with her best friend, Jean Keil, and her parents, who were also motoring to B.C. My memories of the trip are vague except that I sat in the back seat with Aunt Pearl and Mother. Fortunately the weather was nice, so we had the car curtains down the whole time. I don't think any of the roads were paved and we got a fair mixture of dust in the back seat along with the fresh flowing air. The old car didn't do much more than thirty-five miles an hour so we had plenty of time to enjoy the passing scene.

When we finally reached Banff, we were all enchanted by the mountains and the beautiful scenery. The California poppies were in full bloom, and

Stopping at Banff on a trip to visit my grandparents in B.C. (1929).

the big hotel looked like a palace to me. The hot springs and tiled swimming pool were almost beyond anything even I could imagine.

Going through the mountains was very slow, the old car often heating up on the steep inclines on roads that were not much more than narrow trails. On the twisting declines, Mother and Aunt Pearl's feet almost pushed through the floorboards as they prayed for the brakes to hold. It seemed to me that we drove for miles either hugging the rocks on one side or teetering on the edge of a cliff that fell for miles. Finally car sickness overtook me.

My car sickness and the fact that we were not making the time we had expected began to worry Mother. She was sure that at the rate we were travelling we'd never get back in time to allow Lola to get off on her holidays with the Keils. So somewhere in the middle of British Columbia she decided that she and I would catch a train back to Brock. I was very disappointed at not being able to see my grandparents, but once Mother made up her mind there was no changing it. Dad bought our tickets and sent us on our way.

Once during the Depression we did take a week's holidays at Meota on Jackfish Lake, north of North Battleford. The James family lived about four miles from us, and both Mr. and Mrs. James were English. I suspect that Mrs. James, used to holidays by the seashore in England, persuaded Mother it would be a good thing if the two families pooled their resources for a holiday by a lake. Although Meota was probably not much more than a hundred miles away, it seemed to me a very distant and exciting place. We travelled over bumpy gravel roads and Mother kept telling Dad, "Slow down, Alex, you're going too fast."

May Clifford, who was with us, would exclaim with exasperation, "Oh, Lottie, he's only going forty, for heaven's sake. We won't get there till midnight if he slows down!" But Dad would slow down just the same.

The old cottage we rented by the lake was more than rustic, but it did have enough beds to sleep all the James family and us, about thirteen or fourteen people in all. It had a funny old naphtha-gas stove where Mother and Mrs. James prepared our meals, and it was fun sitting down at one big table to eat with our friends.

What I remember best about that short holiday was that I got sick. I couldn't keep any food down and felt miserable. Mrs. James came to my bedside and, putting her hand into her apron pocket, pulled out a small bottle of whiskey and gave me a few sips off a teaspoon. In a short time I was much improved, but couldn't help but wonder, rather guiltily, if my dad

The Meota holiday was taken with the James family in the early 1930s. Above are Don McLean, the hired man who coached Art in pitching ball, Helen, Birdie, and Ruth James. Art, Carf, and I are in front.

knew I'd been cured by the "demon drink" about which he often expounded.

A few years later, when I was twelve or thirteen, the United Church minister, Mr. Miller, decided that some of us kids needed a holiday. This was during the worst part of the Depression, but somehow he rounded up enough money to take about two car loads of us to camp. It was a lovely holiday, like nothing any of us had ever experienced before, with devotions beside a small lake, swimming, hikes, and vespers around a campfire at night. There were lots of highjinks, too, of course, and there may have been times when Mr. Miller wished he hadn't instigated such a plan. Still, I venture to say that none of us who went on that little camping holiday ever forgot it. It was a pleasant oasis in that dry, hot summer.

~

CHAPTER SEVENTEEN

Christmas!

C hristmas! What happy memories the word conjures. Until I left Saskatchewan when I was fifteen, Christmas was spent the same way. Every other year, our family went to the Clendenings', and they would come to our place for New Year's Day. The next year the proceedings were reversed, but the families always celebrated those two important occasions together.

Thoughts of Christmas started back in the fall when the children began preparing the school concert. By the time the date arrived the little ones had reached a feverish pitch, what with the nerve-racking thoughts of performing before an audience and the yearly visit of Santa Claus.

When the concert was finished, a tense hush fell upon us as we strained our ears for the bells that would herald Santa's arrival. Finally, just when we were about to give up, the bells sounded far off in the distance, growing clearer and clearer until the back door burst open and there was Santa, big and jovial, striding down the aisle, jingling a strap of harness bells and ho-ho-hoing his way up to the front. After a short speech about how busy he and his elves were and how he hoped there were not bad boys or girls in the audience, he began to call out our names to come forward to receive our red mesh bags of nuts, candies, and an orange. Sometimes there was another small gift under the tree from our parents, and we often exchanged a present with our best friend, usually something we had made ourselves. Of course we children had no money to buy gifts, but our mothers might come up with an embroidered hankie or a small painted Japanese dish for our teacher. We'd shyly watch her open it and be thrilled with her pleased reaction.

Before I started school, Santa's visit overwhelmed me, and it took a great deal of urging from my mother before I'd walk up to the front with downcast eyes, hardly daring to breathe. I was almost overcome with joy when Santa lifted me up, gave me a hug, and inquired, "Are you sure you've been a good girl, Gwyneth?" I could only nod my head dumbly, thrilled that he remembered my name. It was years before I realized that Santa, with his straggly white whiskers, was my own dear dad in a baggy, faded red suit and rubber boots with the manure scrubbed off.

I was about eight before I found out that Santa Claus was a fairytale, and while I was somewhat let down, it didn't stop me from enjoying the fun of putting up my stocking and the delight of digging out its contents on Christmas morning. Much later, when my own daughter, JoAnne, was in kindergarten, she had a well-meaning but rather strait-laced teacher who sent home a note decrying the "lie" of Santa Claus and asking our permission to tell JoAnne (along with all the other children) the "truth." We said "No!" because we wanted JoAnne to have the same childish, harmless fun her father and I had enjoyed at our Christmases. Times have changed since then, however, and now I have the sinking feeling that the Santa Claus myth has gone too far and that to many children Santa Claus, not the birth of Jesus, is the reason for celebrating Christmas. My friend, the Reverend Barbara Lang, has said that "To many, many children, Santa Claus is the reality, and Jesus is the fairytale."

If that's true, then we Christians had better take pains to make sure our own children and grandchildren know the true meaning of Christmas. I know my friends and I did. At church we took part in special Christmas services and, to the singing of ancient carols and wrapped up in torn sheets and old bathrobes, we acted out the story of Jesus' birth. As the familiar but beautiful story unfolded before our eyes, we felt a close kinship to the holy family, the weary mother, the distraught father, and the tiny baby who had to be born in a cold stable. All of us knew something about hard times ourselves. And we also knew that in some mysterious way we couldn't understand, and in spite of all the hardships of Jesus' family and our own families, God sent down hope and love in that little helpless baby.

When we awakened on Christmas morning we rushed downstairs to find our stockings filled and laid out on the diningroom table. There was no decorated tree. As far as I know, the only Christmas tree in the area was the big one shipped in and put up in the church for the Christmas concert. Mother always made the diningroom look festive by stringing red and green crepe-paper streamers from corner to corner and hanging a red paper foldout bell over the table. After New Year's, these simple decorations were carefully put away for another year.

There was usually a red Delicious apple and a tangerine in the toe of each stocking, along with some fat nuts and brightly coloured hard candy, and likely a gift of something to wear — mitts, a scarf and toque, or new underwear and stockings. I remember when I was about nine how excited I was when I got my first bra for Christmas, which made me feel I was surely (but slowly) growing up!

While we certainly enjoyed our presents, they didn't seem to play as important a role as they do today. I do, however, vividly recall the few occasions when I received books, which were the very best gifts I could ever get. One Christmas, my friend Catherine Jickling gave me *Blackie's Girl Budget*, a big thick book of girls' stories set in remote England which I pored over with great fascination.

A horse-drawn van on sleigh runners carried us over the snow in winter during the Depression.

When it was our turn to go to the Clendenings' for Christmas, we started out in our horse-drawn van about eleven o'clock. It was usually a typical prairie winter's day, clear and cold, with the temperature well below zero on the Fahrenheit scale. We bundled up under the bearskin rug, which weighed us down under its coarse brown and black mottled hair. It always had a faint wild smell about it, reminding me that it had been the skin of a real live black bear roaming around in the north, a rather awesome thought. Our feet were protected from the cold by a thick layer of straw on the floor.

One particularly bright Christmas morning when the horses' breath made clouds on the frigid air and the sun sparkled on the white hoarfrost hanging like thick ropes on barbed-wire fences and telephone wires, there seemed to be a special kind of gladness covering us all. While the horses' bells chimed crisply as we slid along, I cuddled up close to Mother on the hard seat of the van. Suddenly, she bent over and kissed me on the tip of my small nose and hugged me tightly. This was a wonderful, unexpected show of affection from Mother, and a Christmas present that warmed me to my toes. Strangely enough, although she made a great deal of fuss over us and almost loved us to death when we were babies, she always seemed embarrassed to show us too much affection when we grew older — not that we didn't know that she loved us fiercely.

After a half hour's ride over snow-covered fields we arrived at Clendenings', where Earl was waiting with a wide grin to help Dad put the horses in the barn. We stamped into the house, which smelled deliciously of roast turkey, sage dressing, turnips, gravy, and carrot pudding bubbling on the back of the kitchen range. Our faces glowing from the cold as we dropped off our boots and heavy clothes, we called out "Merry Christmas! Merry Christmas!" to a beaming Isabelle, Bubbles, June, and Claude.

Aunt Marion and Uncle Art Cann and our cousin Howard were there too, and shortly fourteen or fifteen of us sat down and devoured the food that loaded the table. In comparison to the elaborate Christmas feasts we have today, I suppose that this Depression dinner was a simple meal. (It wasn't until 1936, when my family motored to Ontario to visit relatives, that I saw an array of food that included three or four different vegetables, two kinds of meat, and several types of salads and condiments all put out at one meal. And the fact that there was usually a layer cake, two kinds of pie, and maple syrup for dessert almost boggled my mind.) Still, it's the memory of those hard-time Christmas dinners eaten around a long table with my loving family and good friends that remains. To a little child they did more than satisfy a zestful appetite; they fed a sense of well-being and security as well.

While the dishes were being washed by Isabelle and Mother with the help of Lola, the boys set up the kitchen chairs in the livingroom for a rousing game of Musical Chairs. Then Isabelle dried her hands, sat down at the old piano, and began a rollicking Irish tune to which the rest of us, young and old alike, marched around the chairs, good naturedly shoving and pushing for a seat when the music stopped. After the last two players had vied for the lone chair, we cheered the winner. Then we pulled the chairs into a circle for a game of Poor Pussy. This was our favorite game, and we children loved nothing better than blindfolding Uncle Art and making him the pussy that crawled around on all fours meowing plaintively before each chair, trying to guess the person who sat there stroking his head and calling in a high falsetto voice, "Poor Pussy!"

Soon Uncle Art, overcome with shaking laughter, collapsed on the floor, to our hilarious delight. When we finally rescued him by taking off the blindfold, he'd pull out his big white hankie to mop up the tears which mixed with the perspiration streaming down his red, crinkled-up face. Then we moved back to the cleared-off diningroom table for a game of Simon Says Thumbs Up, with one of the older children calling the directions and trying to fool us. The afternoon would wind down with games of cards or crokinole before we sat down again and gobbled up a wonderful meal of leftovers.

Too soon it was time to wrap up in our heavy clothes, walk out on the cold scrunchy snow, pile into the old van, and start the trip home through a dark night. The good thing about it was that we knew we were going to repeat the whole performance at our house in a week's time!

The Christmas spirit seemed to last all through January as we went back and forth visiting the other neighbours. One night we'd drive up to the Strutts' in the old van to enjoy a dinner of roast pork and an evening of table games. The next week they'd be back at our place for baked chicken. While our parents visited we kids had some wonderful games of Hide and Seek in the upstairs rooms or took turns sliding down the stair banister.

We went through the same routine with the Salkelds, but the thing I remember most about going to their place was the delicious fried whitefish Laura served in great brown crispy pieces, seasoned exactly right. (In the winter, when there was money, the neighbours went together to ship in several hundredweight of frozen whitefish from northern Saskatchewan.)

Christmases were simple then. We didn't expect many gifts, so we were never disappointed when we didn't get much. Our pleasures were home-made and innocent, but we enjoyed them more than I can say. It was the fun, the love, and the good will shared with family and friends that made Christmas special, and truly merry for a child of the Depression.

~

CHAPTER EIGHTEEN

Mother's Magic Sewing Machine

Every spring when I was little, Mother made up some new outfits for me on her old treadle sewing machine. Her good friend, Isabelle Clendening, sewed for her two little girls, Bubbles and June, so about February she and Mother conferred on the telephone over what material they'd order from the Eaton's catalogue. Having made their decision, they placed the order for which we all waited expectantly.

After the material arrived, the sewing machines whirred for days as the women stitched up dresses for us in cotton print, one of which would be a little fancier than the others for Sunday School. They also swapped patterns, so the Clendening girls and I were often dressed similarly.

One time, when Bubbles and I were five or six, these industrious mothers outdid themselves when they ordered pink, green, and yellow organdy and sewed us fancy frocks with layers of frills ruffling up to our waists. We girls loved these beautiful dresses, but there was a problem: the matching panties.

This was long before polyester, so organdy was not the nice soft stuff it is today. It was stiff and scratchy, and underpants made from it were, to say the least, uncomfortable; in fact, they were unbearable. Bubbles and I discussed the ticklish problem and plot-

Pals forever: Bubbles and I (1928).

90

ted how to get rid of the dreadful things. She was an angelic, chubby-faced little blonde who was never inclined to get into trouble, but those scratchy pants demanded strong action, even from her. She came up with the foolproof solution. We would simply throw them down the hole of the backhouse. Nobody, she said, would ever go down there to get them!

She was right! Although our mothers were cross, and scolded (I'm sure they laughed secretly), they never made us wear organdy pants again.

Mother herself had a marvellous flair for wearing clothes, and no one was more appreciative of her sense of style than Dad. He always accompanied her when she selected a new outfit, his eyes glowing with pride when she picked out something that made her look like a queen.

Before the Depression, about once a year, we went to Saskatoon, travelling the hundred miles by train or, sometimes, in our touring car. In those days, Saskatoon was a small, shabby, pioneer city, not at all like the beautiful place it is today. Yet to us it was as exciting as New York or London. I remember when during the Depression the Bessborough Hotel was built along the banks of the Saskatchewan River as a make-work project. When it was finished, with all its gray stone and many turrets, it looked like something out of a fairytale. I was never inside it until I was in my senior years, it being far too grand for the likes of us, but we did sometimes stay overnight at the modest King George Hotel.

These stays gave Mother plenty of time to peruse all the stores for the latest fashions. She walked miles looking for just the right dress, Dad and I traipsing along in her wake until my little legs gave out. One time I lay down on the floor in a store, stubbornly refusing to budge another inch despite Mother's insistent coaxing, until my soft-hearted Dad picked me up and carried me the rest of the day.

At noon we stopped at a restaurant, and for a little farm girl it was like entering into a strange but enchanting land akin to the make-believe world I inhabited in our back yard. I remember one place especially, a Chinese restaurant with gleaming black wood, red velvet drapes that partitioned off the small cubicles, and smiling slant-eyed men who glided silently over the floor. The tables were covered with heavy damask cloths and there were white starched napkins folded into fans at every setting. Mother tucked mine under my chin to keep my best dress clean while I ate from green-rimmed porcelain plates with polished silverware. My eyes feasted on the surroundings so that I scarcely knew what I was eating, and when at the end of the meal the Chinese waiter brought us each a hammered brass bowl of warm water, I was greatly surprised, as I was about to drink mine, to hear Mother smilingly inform me that it was for washing off my sticky hands.

On some occasions when Dad wasn't able to go to the city with us, Mother and I put up in May Clifford's tiny flat, Mother sleeping on a cot and me on the floor. It wasn't nearly as exciting as the hotel, but it gave Mother and May a chance to catch up on their visiting. I hugged my pillow and drifted off to sleep to the sound of their happy chattering.

When the Depression struck, getting food on your plate was the first priority. Getting an education for your children was second, while putting clothes on their back came in third. Trips to the city came in last.

When there was no money to send for material from Eaton's catalogue, Mother kept us clothed by mending and re-mending and cutting up her old coats and Dad's suits to make them down to fit us. They may not always have looked like the pictures in the catalogue over which we pored, but they kept us covered and warm.

In 1930, when Lola was seventeen, she was ready to go to Normal School (Teacher's College) in Saskatoon, and Dad and Mother faced the seemingly insuperable odds of finding the money to send her. They talked long into the night trying to figure out how they could possibly raise funds for tuition and board. Although it seemed impossible, Mother's determination never flagged. Lola would go to Saskatoon even if the rest of us starved a little.

So Dad hauled out ten loads of our precious wheat at around twenty cents a bushel to make up the two hundred dollars needed for tuition. Where the year's board money would come from, however, they couldn't venture to guess, but they waved her off anyway, having faith that, somehow, they would manage it. And somehow they always did, scratching up the necessary twenty dollars by the end of every month.

However, even if tuition and board could be looked after, there was certainly no money for clothes. Mother knew, though, that a young girl going off to the city had to have decent things to wear. There were still some yards of white wool serge in the trunk she'd brought from Ontario years before, and luckily she could perform miracles at the sewing machine. The dress she designed, with its red, silk-lined cape, would have made Christian Dior weep with envy. Then she ripped apart many of her own better clothes and some of Dad's as well, recutting and remaking until Lola's wardrobe could have taken her anywhere. Mother's reward was sufficient when she heard that her daughter was one of the smartest-dressed girls in the school. Later, with a twinkle in his eye, Dad would recount, "You know, I never knew if I'd find my duds hanging in the closet or on Lola's back!"

When times grew worse, the trips to Saskatoon were less frequent, although Mother sometimes still went in for a day's outing with Isabelle. Even if they couldn't afford to purchase new dresses, they still enjoyed looking at the clothes in the stores, and picked up ideas about how to revamp their old garments.

Sometimes we shopped in Kindersley, a largish town about twenty miles away, and when I was thirteen Mother bought me my first "store" dress there. It was a rather plain, rust-coloured crepe frock with a shiny pin at the neck, and although I thought it was the most beautiful thing I had ever put on my back, I know now that it wasn't nearly as pretty as some of the dresses Mother made over for me from old clothes sent by her sisters in Ontario. She could work magic with a discarded garment, cutting it apart and turning it into a dress of the latest fashion. She was simply the most talented seamstress I have ever known, and had it not been for her genius we would not have had the clothes we wore during the Depression.

When I went back to the Brock School Reunion, one of the girls I hadn't seen for forty years said to me, "What I remember about you is the nice clothes your mother made for you!" It was a compliment, and I thanked her on behalf of my mother.

~

CHAPTER NINETEEN

Fun in the straw: Carf, Marjorie Allen, me, Audrey Allen, Jean Keil, and Art.

Birthdays and Straw Stacks

Birthdays are strange! At ten years, I dreamed of being thirteen, when I'd leave childhood behind. But when I did reach thirteen, it seemed that sixteen was the age when you started to have fun. Then eighteen loomed enticingly ahead, the door to freedom and adulthood, but having attained eighteen years, I found I wasn't considered an adult until I "came of age" at twenty-one and could cast my vote. After that, the years flew by and the birthdays piled up more quickly than I wanted them to.

As my birthdays have come and gone, there's one that has stood out like a beacon: my eighth. Until then I had never had a birthday party. Oh, there were always candles on a cake with nickels and pennies hidden inside at the supper table, but never a bona fide party. One of the reasons for this was that my birthday fell on Hallowe'en when there always seemed to be enough excitement as we children, and often the adults too, dressed up in old clothes and called on the neighbours for great chunks of homemade fudge or toffee.

Carf and Art told me it was the witches (instead of the stork) that brought me, and that some Hallowe'en they would fly back and pick me up again. When I was very small they'd whisper in my ear, "Maybe it's *this* Hallowe'en," and I'd be so scared I couldn't enjoy my birthday. Mother didn't help much. She loved to put on a dough face, pull an old toque over her head, and run around outside the house, rapping on the windows, woo-oo-ing painfully. I sat on Dad's knee, my arms tight around his neck, because even though I knew it was really Mother and kind of enjoyed the tingles going up and down my back, there was always the chance it just might be a witch fulfilling my brothers' prophecy.

94

A bumper crop in the 1920s. All grain was stooked in those days.

By the time I was eight, I didn't believe in witches anymore, but I did want a birthday party. When I timidly broached the subject, Mother looked doubtful, but Dad, listening in the background, hit on a marvellous idea. "We could burn that straw stack in the north field," he twinkled.

Burn a straw stack for my birthday! That was more than I could ever have hoped for, and Mother, seeing Dad bracing up my expectation, acquiesced gracefully.

This was when grain was cut close to the ground, bound into sheaves by a binder, and then separated by a threshing machine. Men forked the sheaves into the grinding jaws of this machine which, in a most miraculous operation (or so it seemed to me), caused the wheat kernels to flow like a golden river through a pipe into waiting wagons while the straw was chopped up and blown out into large stacks.

In the early days, Dad and his brother Lawrence owned a "threshing outfit" and threshed the grain of all the farmers in the neighbourhood. The outfit travelled from field to field led by a huge black locomotive pulling the lumbering, silver-coloured threshing machine, the bunkhouse where the hired hands slept, and the cook car with its smoke stack puffing happily. Next came the teams of horses pulling the stook loader, the high-racked wagons for the sheaves, and the wagons with the narrow boxes to hold the threshed grain.

It was quite a cavalcade. Grandma Cann, Mother, or Aunt Marion (Uncle Art's wife) rode along in the cook car, preparing all the meals for the hungry

The harvest cavalcade: Dad and Uncle Lawrence's threshing outfit travelled from farm to farm. Behind the separator is the cook house and bunkhouse.

threshers. Lola remembers going along when she was little and sleeping in a bed made up on the floor under the planks that served as tables.

By my time, however, Dad was running the outfit by himself, and while the stook loader and wagons still followed the tractor and threshing machine from farm to farm, the bunkhouse remained on our property and Mother served the men their breakfasts and suppers at our stretched-out diningroom table. When they were working on our own farm, she fed them all their meals, but usually the wife of the farmer who was having his crop threshed supplied the noonday dinner.

Everything geared up for harvest and it was an exciting time. Extra help was needed, so Dad went to town to hire "hands." Most of these were clean-cut young men from the East who dropped off the train looking for a bit of adventure and some money to take home. Occasionally, however, we got some duds, like the time our full-time hired man, Lorne Little, brought home three wild characters who were more interested in drinking "canned heat" than in putting in a day's work. They and Dad soon parted company.

Another time, when help was hard to find, Dad hired a surly, rough-looking fellow who almost scared Mother to death. His table manners were non-existent as he hunched over his food like some angry black bear, never passing anything to anyone else. And although his clothes were filthy, they were nothing compared to the language that flowed from his mouth. I'm sure the man was deranged, and when Dad finally fired him Mother was terrified that he'd come back and murder us in our beds.

One day, another strange-looking fellow arrived looking for work. He

Harvesting the crop.

was squat, burly, and uncommunicative, with eyes hidden behind very thick steel-rimmed glasses. One morning the other men came in for breakfast with the news that "Joe" was sick. This went on for three days, and although Mother offered to send food to the bunkhouse, word always came back that Joe didn't want any. Finally on the afternoon of the fourth day he came staggering into the kitchen where Mother and Birdie James, the young girl who helped with the cooking and washing up at harvest time, were preparing the afternoon lunch for the threshers. For some reason or other, Art was home from school, and he and I were off in a corner where he was teaching me how to play Cat's Cradle with a piece of string.

Joe, ghastly pale, his thick, unruly hair falling over his face and his clothes in disarray, looked like an almost dead scarecrow. Mother, not knowing exactly what was wrong with him and thinking he might be getting over a drinking binge, was very nervous over his appalling appearance, but she did offer to make him a cup of tea when he slumped into a chair.

He sat at the table, his head in his arms, not moving or speaking,until she placed the steaming cup in front of him. Then, as he lifted it with shaking hands to take his first sip, his large head crashed to the table, sending dishes clattering and tea spraying in every direction while he fell heavily to the floor, his chair banging down on top of him. Mother let out a terrified scream, dropped the teapot, and flew for the door. Poor surprised Birdie, taking her cue from Mother, screamed and flew after her. Art, caught for a moment in the entanglement of Cat's Cradle, ripped his fingers away from the string, leapt over the man, and also bolted for the open door. Deserted, and left alone with the heavy figure sprawled on the kitchen floor, was more than enough to convince me that this was no place to be, so I raced after them, bawling lustily.

The unfortunate man had only fainted from weakness, and by the time Mother had collected her courage to go back into the house, he was picking himself up off the floor. Sheepishly, she made him another cup of tea and advised him to go back to the bunkhouse and lie down while we took the lunch to the men in the fields.

I loved this break. The engine was shut down for fifteen minutes while Dad and the men gathered round for a brief rest and some nourishment to carry them through till evening. Mother baked a big batch of her light-as-a-feather tea biscuits (one appreciative man declared they were food for the angels) and

Uncle Art Cann and the stook loader. Our house is in the background at the right.

spread them with jam and honey. These were wolfed down with the warm sweet tea she ladled from a big preserving kettle.

While the men sat on the ground enjoying their lunch and a brief rest from the hard work, I'd climb up on a grain wagon and grab a handful of raw wheat. Tossing it into my mouth, I'd chew until it turned into a kind of mushy gum, not exactly Wriggley's Spearmint, but good nonetheless.

The work went on in the fields from early morning until six or seven in the evening. Then the men unhitched their teams and drove them back to the barn. Dad made sure the help he hired never mistreated his horses. Every evening they were thoroughly combed and curried, watered and fed, and bedded down in fresh straw before the men sloshed the dirt off their own faces at the well. With good-natured bantering they tramped into the house, still digging the straw out of their necks, for a hearty supper of roast beef, fried potatoes, mashed turnips, cabbage salad, and two or three kinds of pie.

Some of the straw from the great stacks in the fields was hauled to the barn for feed and bedding. What was left over was set aflame, making a stupendous bonfire which could be seen for miles. It was always an event, but on my eighth birthday it was more than that, it was a stupendous occasion!

On a clear, frosty, moonless October night, we congregated in the middle of a hundred-acre field around a mammoth stack of straw. All the neighbours were there — moms, dads, children of all ages. I also invited some school chums, my teacher, the minister and his family, and two bachelors, Bert and Dick, whom everyone invited to everything. Unadulterated joy pulsed through my small, shivering frame.

Some of the straw was pulled from the stack and set on fire to give light and warmth for the adults who huddled around rubbing their hands over the heat. We children didn't need anything to keep us warm; by the light of the small fire and in dark, changing shadows we climbed up the soft mountain, sinking to our knees. Over and over we tumbled down its glossy sides amid hoots of laughter and flailing arms and legs. The scratchy straw pushing down our necks and sticking in our hair didn't deter the fun for a moment.

Just when we were beginning to reach exhaustion, Dad called us off the stack for the main event. Taking a shovel of burning straw from the small fire, he skirted the stack, setting it ablaze in several places. Because it was loose and dry, it became, almost at once, a towering, blazing, yellow and gold inferno flaring high into the black night, the glowing sparks and white smoke spiralling to meet the stars.

We stood mesmerized as the brilliant leaping flames turned dark night into bright day, pushing us back with their searing heat. The stack burned inside its cone until it collapsed into a red heaving mass of coals, the pungent smoke filling our nostrils.

Meanwhile, Mother had unpacked the lunch, and we sat on blankets close enough to the fire to be warm but not so close that we would get scorched, gobbling up thick egg sandwiches and drinking cups of steaming cocoa from a big aluminum pot. A colossal chocolate cake appeared, its eight tiny, trembling candles dwarfed by the giant bonfire. Mother scooped cake into our bare hands and we licked the sticky sweet icing off our fingers while our dreamy eyes reflected the fire.

One of the bachelors got out his mouth organ and haunted the night with "The Wreck of the Old Forty-Nine," "Home, Home on the Range," and other plaintive cowboy tunes. As the last bittersweet glow of the fire faded, parents prodded reluctant children off blankets to head them, trance-like, for home.

There's never been another party like it. I was amazed when I went back to the school reunion at how many people came up to me and remarked with a faraway look in their eyes, "Remember the night we burned the straw stack on your birthday?" It had been a memorable occasion for them, too.

~

CHAPTER TWENTY

No Malpractice

W|e lived in the Rural Municipality of Hillsburgh, and in 1920 it became either the first or one of the first municipalities in the country to implement free medical services to its residents. It was a system that worked wonderfully well. The council simply hired a doctor and nurse to look after all the medical needs of the sick, young and old, rich and poor, and paid their wages from the taxes. The levy for this service was five dollars per quarter section of land.

Although Hillsburgh was sparsely populated, it was a large area, taking in more than three hundred square miles, and the doctor often had to travel a long distance to reach his patients. In the summer he bumped along the narrow roads in a Model T, but in the winter he had to rely on his trusty little horse to pull him through the snow drifting across the prairie while he bundled up in the cutter under his bearskin rug.

The municipal doctor and nurse were greatly respected in the community. They worked as a team, moving into a house where someone was critically ill and working long hours until the crisis passed. Then the doctor returned home, leaving the nurse to care for the patient and, if the patient happened to be a mother, to look after the rest of her family. Despite their limited resources, this team brought many people through grave illnesses. They had their failures, of course, but no one ever suggested they hadn't done everything in their power to save the life of a sick person. Malpractice hadn't even been thought of in those days.

When we were ill, we were, like everyone else, looked after in our own houses, and if it wasn't serious enough for a doctor's visit Mother simply rang him up, described the symptoms, and followed his instructions with tender loving care which, when we were little, included a large dose of being rocked in her old rocking chair.

One time when a little boy from town was visiting us, he suddenly fell to the floor in a convulsion, his body jerking and his eyes rolling back in his head. I was terrified, and even Mother hadn't seen anything like this before, so she ran to the phone and called the doctor, who told her to bathe the child with cold cloths. The poor little fellow soon came round again, but Mother held him in her arms and crooned him to sleep as she rocked back and forth to the soothing creak of the chair.

Occasionally Mother was the patient herself, a bad case of flu or a severe sinus headache forcing her to bed. The whole world seemed to go out of kilter when Mother was sick: the food didn't taste as good, the house was never as tidy, and the very air had a sombre feeling about it. It wasn't until she was up and around again that the cloud lifted and things started to click along normally once more.

She was the kind that fainted rather easily, although on at least one occasion she had plenty of reason. Running quickly down the stairs one night with her hand on the banister, her finger hit a loosened splinter, which sank deeply into her fingernail — almost to the first joint. Carf, about thirteen at the time, heard her calling for help and rushed down to find her leaning against the wall, her finger spurting a fountain of blood. "Quick," she gasped, "Get the pliers!" He ran to Dad's toolbox, picked up the pliers, and somehow got hold of the tip of the thick sliver sticking out the end of Mother's finger. Slowly he pulled it out while she fainted dead away at his feet. Why she never got lockjaw or blood poisoning was a miracle.

It was Carf, when he was in his late teens, who turned out to be the one who got blood poisoning. A blister had formed on the palm of his hand when he was pumping up a car tire. He didn't bother to bandage it or even apply iodine, and when it broke it became infected. As blood poisoning took hold, his hand swelled up to the size of a small football, his fingers sticking out like fat, stiff sausages and an angry red line advancing up his arm. This was long before sulpha and penicillin, and blood poisoning was a serious matter. The doctor was very concerned when he couldn't get the red line to recede. Finally he lanced the hand, making two great cuts like a cross on Carf's swollen palm to release the pus. There was talk that the arm might have to be amputated and for several hours Carf's very life hung in the balance. He sat with his poison-filled hand in a pail of hot salty water until, finally, the red line began to move down his arm. The crisis was over, but it had been a scary time for all of us.

We kids picked up all the contagious diseases that came around, but I particularly remember when I had the red measles. Both Carf and Lola were away when the epidemic broke out at school, but it wasn't long before Art came down with them and was put to bed. When several days had passed, it looked as if I might be going to escape, but there came a night when I was going to bed that I didn't feel very well.

Early next morning I had a terrible dream. I dreamt that our cross Hereford bull (of which I was terrified) was chasing me around and around the barnyard. Frantically trying to escape, I ran and ran, but he kept gaining on me, snorting and puffing and kicking up dirt angrily. Eventually I reached the fence, but just when I went to duck under it to safety I became entangled in the barbed wire. I was wringing with sweat as I desperately tried to tear my clothes from the wire, feeling the bull's hot breath upon me and expecting his horns and hooves to tear me to shreds. I screamed and woke up.

Mother came running. My pyjamas and sheets were soaking wet with perspiration, and I was covered with red measles from head to toe.

In those days, it was thought that strong light weakened the eyes of anyone with measles. So Mother drew all the blinds and warned me that I was in no way to try to read. But it was too much to ask. I couldn't lie there doing nothing, so I decided just a little reading wouldn't hurt. I sneaked out of bed, got a book, and if I squinted up my eyes I could make out the words in the semi-darkness. I had to be careful, though, that Art, who was still sick in the next room, didn't get up and catch me, for I knew he would surely tell.

I soon remembered that Dad kept an old flashlight in his dresser drawer, so I crept out and got it and then pulled the blankets over my head to read in peace under the covers. The book was one May Clifford had discarded from the library in Saskatoon. It was a romance novel, *Henry of Navarre*, quite racy to my young mind, and my eyes couldn't devour the pages fast enough. Since Mother had no time to read herself, she had no idea of the contents, but had she known she would have been aghast. Before long she did discover me under the covers with the flashlight, and all light and books were completely banned from my room. It was only for a few days, but it seemed like an eternity.

A couple of years later, when I complained of not being able to see the school blackboard, she had no sympathy, saying I had only myself to blame. Actually, she and Dad didn't take me seriously when I insisted I couldn't see properly. They thought my wanting glasses was just the passing fancy of a thirteen-year-old. Finally I persuaded Dad to take me to a doctor in Eston who did eye tests. I remember Dad's complete astonishment when the test proved I was very near-sighted. "I thought she was only fooling when she almost had to put her nose on the chart before she could read it," he confessed to Mother that night.

A couple weeks later, the round steel-rimmed glasses arrived in the mail in a little cardboard box. I unwrapped them carefully from the tissue paper and gingerly set them on my nose. An explosion of sight burst before me.

I ran to the window, almost unable to believe that the thick fog I was accustomed to looking through had dissipated like magic. The clump of maple trees that had been just a fuzzy mass now had definite shapes with limbs and branches and leaves. The barn and outbuildings moved into sharp focus, and I could see things I'd forgotten were there. "I didn't know there was a granary in Berrows' field." I turned to Mother, who was standing at my side. "And look, I can see the cows out in the pasture, and the slaughter-house, and Strutts' place up the road!"

She thought I was teasing, took the glasses off my eyes, and placed them over her own. There was a moment's silence as the shock that these were very strong lenses indeed sank in. Slowly she handed them back to me. "Oh, Gwyneth," she cried with tears in her eyes, "we didn't know your sight was so bad. You should have had glasses long ago."

I shall never forget the difference those spectacles made in my life, and to this day my glasses are my most protected and valued possession. I fail to understand when I hear some people complaining because they have to wear glasses. As for me, I continually thank God that there are glasses available for people like me who have eye problems.

Mother never got it out of her head that I had ruined my eyes when I had measles. I think another incident might have had more to do with it.

Minor operations, including the removal of tonsils and adenoids and sometimes even appendicitis operations, were done at home. As a young child I had a nasty nasal and throat problem, which Dr. Black said was catarrh. About a year after I had the measles, he suggested to my parents that I have my tonsils and adenoids taken out. Of course there was no hospital, but his nurse, May Strong, had a large bright kitchen that he sometimes used as his operating theatre.

Mrs. Strong and her husband lived above the grocery store they operated, and Dad deposited me there on a certain morning around ten o'clock. I was nervous to start with, but when I saw the kitchen table, which I knew to be the site of the operation, covered with thick layers of blankets, an uncontrolled shiver of terror ran through my small frame.

Mother taught us all to be stoics, and if we hurt ourselves or were afraid we were supposed to buck up and not cry. She might have had many fears and misgivings herself, but the thing was to keep all your feelings under cover. I'm sure she was very concerned about my operation, but she built me up with the idea that it was a high adventure from which I would not only come out the victor, but much healthier too. I found it hard to remember all this as my knees wobbled and knocked together and my teeth chattered when the doctor and nurse helped me up to the kitchen table.

"You aren't afraid, are you?" the doctor asked me kindly.

"No," I lied as my heart pounded wildly and my hands clutched the blankets.

He leaned over me and showed me a gauze-covered, cone-like affair that he said he was going to place over my mouth and nose. "Nurse Strong will drop of few drops of ether on the cone, and soon you'll be fast asleep. When you wake up, your tonsils and adenoids will be gone."

He put the cone over my face. I began to panic. "Relax," he said calmly and gently. "Now, start to count for me."

"One, two, three ..." The sweet smell of ether filled my nostrils. I breathed deeply. "Four, five ..." The world began to whirl round and round faster and faster, spinning down into a deep black hole. Then nothing.

The next thing I knew Nurse Strong was calling my name, telling me the operation was over. Although I was terribly sick and groggy, I felt a great surge of relief that I was still alive, and fell back to sleep.

Shortly after, Dad came, carefully picked me up, and carried me down to the car where Mother was waiting. They laid me on pillows on the back seat. For some reason I couldn't open my eyes, but I was too sick and too tired to worry about it.

It was wonderful to be laid in my own bed, to feel the cool sheets under me. As I became more conscious, I realized my eyes were bandaged, but in a little while Lola tiptoed into my room and took them off. She told me she had some drops to put in my eyes, which were burning like fire.

It seems that after I had lost consciousness, but while the ether was still dropping on the mask, my hand had suddenly shot up, knocking the cone and the ether container flying. Some of it had spilled on my face and in my eyes, burning both.

I guess I was lucky I didn't lose my sight. In a week or so the burns had pretty well healed, and the doctor assured my parents that my eyes were OK. Nevertheless, I imagine they were damaged more than he or they suspected at the time.

The doctors and nurses of that era often had to work under conditions that were much less than ideal, and if sometimes they made mistakes, who could blame them? After all, they were only human. Today, looking back from this very scientific age to that primitive operation, I can still attach no blame to anyone for what happened, but have always believed that this was the main cause of the deterioration of my sight.

If medical care was less than perfect, dentistry during the '20s and '30s in rural areas could be almost uncivilized. The nearest dentist lived in Kindersley, and that seemed a long way to go with a toothache. Besides, there was the cost to consider, so the municipal doctor was usually called upon to pull the offending tooth to relieve the throbbing pain.

Mother had trouble with her teeth from time to time, and on more than one occasion had to have one pulled by the doctor. One time when several of her molars were causing her a great deal of pain, Dr. Johnson suggested that they be removed while she was under anesthetic.

On the appointed day, she lay on the couch in our kitchen while he dropped ether on the mask covering her face until she was unconscious. The molars were deeply rooted and hard to pull, and Dad had to administer a few more drops of ether whenever Mother began to stir to consciousness. Examining Mother's front teeth, the doctor detected several in various states of decay. "I think I might as well take out all her teeth now, and have it over with," he said to Dad. And I guess Dad agreed.

When Mother awoke and found she was missing all her teeth and not just her molars, her anger knew no bounds. Even though she was feeling pretty sick, she raved the doctor out of the house and was even crosser with Dad for agreeing with the doctor. She scolded him for days.

I suspect her vanity was hurt as much as anything because she had to go toothless for a long time, waiting for her gums to heal so she could be fitted with false teeth. But when she finally got used to her new teeth she was delighted with them. It was wonderful not to be bothered with any more toothaches and she admitted to Dad that he and the doctor had made a good decision after all.

I had a few baby teeth pulled by one of my brothers who tied a string around them and attached the other end of the string to a door knob. One good slam of the door and the tooth was out. But when one of my permanent molars developed a black spot when I was about eight, Mother was most anxious that I have it repaired. It happened that a travelling dentist got off the train at Brock one evening and set up his office in a room at the hotel, so it was arranged that I go to him and have my molar filled.

Since it was during school hours, I had to be excused. I walked slowly down the board sidewalk to the hotel, and the climb up the hotel stairs seemed very long to my weak knees. When I reached the second floor, the sombre-faced dentist was waiting, motioning me to hurry. Although I'd never seen a dentist before, I didn't think he looked like much of one with his wispy gray hair falling over his forehead and ears, his long skinny fingers yellowed with nicotine, and his rough brown coat smelling strongly of tobacco. I've never been able to decide if he was a saint travelling to remote areas to save children's teeth or if he was a charlatan who played on the conditions of rural people.

In any event, he was about as jolly as a hangman, and as he seated me on an ordinary high-backed chair with two pillows to raise me up and another at the back of my head, I thought I knew exactly how the hangman's victim felt.

"Here," he said gruffly, "Play with this." And he poured some quicksilver into my shaking palm. I had never seen quicksilver before, and for a few moments I was fascinated as the little balls rolled around, dividing and then coming together again. Then, abruptly, "Open wide," he commanded.

How I withstood the ordeal I'll never tell you. There was no electricity, so he used a treadle drill worked by his foot as a sewing machine would be, which was anything but smooth. And of course there was no freezing, and the grinding pain was more excruciating than anything I had ever felt before as the whirring old drill bit savagely into my tooth. I was as wild-eyed with panic as any of the steers ever herded into my dad's slaughterhouse.

Somehow I was able to hold back the tears, and finally the drilling was over. I smelt the strong, pungent odour of oil of cloves as he dabbed my open tooth with cotton batting. Then he mixed up the filling with his fingers and pushed it into the hole. I slid from the chair, let the quicksilver drop to the floor, fished his two-dollar fee from my pocket, and ran for the door.

It was years before I could be persuaded to visit a dentist again, but I did spend much more time diligently cleaning my teeth. Yet I must give that old-time dentist his due; fifty-five years later, I still have that filling.

~

CHAPTER TWENTY-ONE

Brothers: Teasers and Protectors

A s youngsters, my brothers were inseparable. Whenever we thought of one, we included the other. It was never just Carf, or just Art, but always Carf *and* Art. When I was still learning to talk, their friends loved to ask me my brothers' names to hear me lisp innocently, "Carss and Arss."

Although there were occasions when I ran crying to Mother because "Bad Carss and Arss" were teasing me, there were many times when they allowed me to snuggle down between them in their warm bed, and days when they were uncommonly tolerant and kind about letting their little sister trail along — even when they went gopher hunting.

Gophers thrived on the dry prairies, reproducing in large colonies in burrows connected by tunnels. Because they were a frightful bane, devouring grain and greatly reducing the yield of crops, the municipal government offered a bounty for

"Carss" (right) and "Arss" with their faithful dog Tiny (1926).

their tails. During the Depression, it was only half a cent per tail, but even this amount was a welcome gift to canny entrepreneurs like Carf and Art, who enjoyed having a little change jingling in their pockets.

There were many ways to acquire gopher tails. One was to shoot the little rodents with a 22 rifle, but shells cost money and eliminated the profit. If a slough or well was close by, you could pour pails of water into their holes until they came up for air and your trusty dog made short work of them. Or, you could snare them with a long piece of bindertwine. This last method was favoured by my brothers, but it required a great deal of patience to outwit and outwait a chary gopher. The boys used a piece of twine about fifteen feet long and made a slip noose at one end which they placed carefully over the gopher hole. Then they lay flat on the ground holding fast the far end of the twine and waited, staring intently at the hole, not daring to move a muscle. When I was allowed to lie beside them, if I happened to sneeze or even scratch my ear I was immediately banned from the hunt and sent back to the house with a severe scolding ringing in my ears. However, if we waited long enough and quietly enough, the curiosity of the gopher was bound to get the better of him, and he'd cautiously poke his head out of the hole. His beady eyes locked with the unblinking eyes of the boy whose hand tightened on the string but still didn't move. The gopher, becoming more daring, came out a little farther until his neck and front legs were showing. Then, without warning, the boy jerked the string, felt the noose tighten around the small body, and pulled it from the hole, grinning triumphantly and one half cent richer!

Some of Art and Carf's friends insisted that if you cut the tail of a gopher it would grow another one. But my brothers always dispatched the little beasts with a quick blow to the head because they knew if Dad ever found out they had cut the tail off before they killed the animal, they would certainly be in for it!

Sometimes, when they were at school, I tried my own luck at snaring gophers, but I usually didn't have the patience, and once when I actually did catch one I couldn't bring myself to kill it, so let it race off trailing the long string behind it. I don't know what the animal rights people would say about the methods used to kill gophers back in those days, but to us it was as natural as breathing to get rid of the pests eating our father's crops any way we could.

I was always intrigued by the other animals that the boys added to their wide collection of pets. They had the usual ones found on a farm — kittens, dogs, horses, calves, and even pigs — but they were always picking up a wild baby animal that had strayed from its mother and was too young to fear humans. There were many baby rabbits, bundles of soft gray fluff with tiny black twitching noses and powder-puff tails. When we stroked the rabbits gently, their little black ears lay back flat on their heads as they cuddled up against us. One grew into a huge, tame fellow who had the run of the house until one day he leapt out the window and was gone, back to his natural habitat.

Another time the boys had a badger named Billy who grew fat and full-grown with long gray hair, a white blaze down his back, and a small, pointed black head. Although badgers ate mice and gophers, they were still a menace to farmers because they burrowed large holes in the fields and caused great danger to horses who might step into one of the holes and break a leg. But Billy seemed harmless enough living in an empty wheat granary and tamed by Carf and Art to the point where he grew very lazy.

One day, his young keepers decided that they should give him a change and allow him to roam outside. Afraid he might run away, they made a little collar for him from a bit of leather strap and tethered him to a post. Imagine their surprise when he shuffled to the end of his rope and simply hunched his shoulders so that the collar popped right over his head. They hadn't realized that Billy's neck was larger than his head and that he was a talented escape artist.

Sometimes the boys even brought home sharp-face coyote puppies they found in a den in the field. But these little fellows never seemed to become tame or gentle, and Mother and Dad usually persuaded the boys to take them back to where they had found them. A coyote was the last animal I wanted for a pet. I was terrified of them. Many a dark night I lay trembling in my bed listening to the mournful Yac, Yac, Yac, Ou-ah-oo-oo-ahhh which raised the hair on the back of my neck and sent tingles down my spine into my toes. Usually one lone animal started the wail, but before long it would be joined by the distant, singing call of many others, growing louder and louder until it seemed there were a dozen circling right around the house, defying anyone to come out. They often did in fact come so close and make so much noise with their plaintive howling that Dad, to stop the fearful bedlam, had to get up and send a shattering blast from his old shotgun into the black night.

If anyone hated coyotes more than I, it was our old dog, Wallace. And not much wonder. They loved to tease him and often sent one of the pack to the edge of the barnyard, even in daylight, to challenge him to a fight. Wallace never turned them down and, screaming with rage, bounded after the cunning coyote that loped ahead just fast enough to keep out of reach. As soon as the coyote lured Wallace over the hill and out of our sight, he was joined by two or three of his mangy friends who, snarling and growling, circled the poor old dog. Wallace stood firm with bared fangs, taking them all on, but it was an unfair fight, and soon he was forced to retreat, his white coat stained with blood while the savage scalawags howled and taunted him derisively. He never did learn, or give up. After a few days of resting and licking his wounds he'd be back chasing them over the hill again and ready for another mismatched, bloody battle.

Coyotes were a constant worry to Mother because they loved to raid her chicken and turkey pens. Although old Wallace always sounded the alarm when they got too close, giving us time to rush out and chase them away, it was inevitable that one or two of the birds would escape from their pen and stray into coyote territory, never to be seen again. Dad would point out the moral of the occasion by reciting a poem he had learned by heart as a small schoolboy.

> Once a little turkey, fond of her own way
> Wouldn't ask the old one where to go or stay.
> She said, "I'm not a baby, here I am half grown,
> Surely I am big enough to run about alone."
> So, off she went; but someone hiding saw her pass,
> And soon her snow-white feathers covered all the grass,
> For she made a supper for a sly young mink
> Because she was so headstrong that she didn't think.

The pets we all loved best were the wild baby ducks. Every spring, flocks of ducks arrived from the north by the hundreds, settling down on the fields and breaking up into pairs to breed and nest. Often they built their nests in fields of long stubble which had to be plowed down for spring seeding or cultivated for summer fallow.

After the pair pressed straw into a strongly molded nest lined with down from their own bodies, the female laid a dozen or more light green eggs. She sat so still in the straw stubble that she was almost invisible, but Dad was always on the lookout for nests when he was cultivating a field. As the horses approached, there would be a sudden wild flight of the mother duck, who would quack loudly and flop along the ground as if her wing was broken, trying to draw attention away from her eggs. Dad would get down and search until he found the hidden nest and would carefully lift it to safe ground already cultivated. Usually the mother finished the job of incubating the eggs, but sometimes, if the nest had been ripped up or destroyed, Dad brought the undamaged eggs home and placed them under a clucky hen. Then came the exciting period of waiting for Old Mother Nature to decide which would be hatched first, the baby ducks or the hen's own chicks. This hatching and raising of wild ducklings and baby chicks together was an enchanting experience for us children.

My brothers taught me many things, amoung them how to ride a horse,

110

hoisting me up on the broad backs of the work horses almost as soon as I could walk. They had their own steeds and were good riders, and although I never became as expert as they, I still loved to mount up on old Jack for a canter across the country — providing he was in the mood, of course! He was the most stubborn, pig-headed, belligerent horse on the face of the earth, and when I was very young and wanted to go for a ride he thought nothing of bucking me off if he didn't choose to go outside the gate. Because he was a tall horse I had to lead him to a fencepost so I could climb onto his back again. But as soon as I went to mount him he simply moved away so that I slid down his side, landing on the hard ground beneath him. Though I screamed and even kicked his shins on more than a few occasions, he would not let me get on again. Finally I'd

My brothers boosted me up on a horse as soon as I could walk.

holler for Dad, who would come, laughing, with a small switch in his hand. He'd jump on Jack's back, touch him lightly with the switch, and the horse would run through the gate like it was the only thing he had on his mind. Turning him back, Dad would hand me the switch and lift me up on Jack's back, telling me, "You've got to let him know who's boss. Dig in your heels and give him the switch." So I'd do all that and Jack would saunter out the gate until we were out of Dad's sight and then he'd turn around and start for home again. Taking Dad's advice, I'd kick his sides as hard as I could and bring the switch down on his withers. Even then, Jack often didn't pay more attention to me than he would to a small fly on his rump, and even if he did decide to go in the direction I wanted him to he always moved in a slow sideways walk, just so we both knew who really was boss!

As I grew older and stronger, I had a little more control over him, but not much. He was loathe to leave the farm, preferring to dream along the fence in the barnyard, and I still had to switch him to make him go through the gate. But oh how he loved to come home. As soon as I turned his face back towards the farm there was no holding him as he raced across the fields, his body stretched out like Northern Dancer's. One time when I was out riding with Art and a group of friends, it came time to head for home and Jack took off like a shot out of a gun, leaving all the other horses far behind and me hanging on for dear life, my jacket flying out behind. After this wild ride I was nicknamed John Gilpin, a moniker I hated.

Once home, Jack was never fully content until he was back in his stall with his long velvety nose nuzzling his manger full of oats. One day, even though I was still on his back, and even though the barn door was only partly open, he insisted on squeezing his way through, crushing my ankle between the stirrup and the door. I still have the scar to prove it, but for some reason or other I loved that horse.

I was not the only victim of old Jack's skulduggery. He was a spoiled animal who thought hard work far beneath him. Only at harvest time, when Dad might need an extra horse, was he ever hitched up to a wagon. If the driver happened to be a greenhorn from the city who was unaccustomed to the wiles of a horse like Jack, he was in for a bad time because Jack would do everything in his power to make the poor man's life miserable.

One day an inexperienced hand tried to hitch him up with another horse, but nothing could convince Jack to move into position so the harness could be hooked to the whipple tree. Though the man begged, pushed, and pulled, Jack refused to budge. Losing his temper, the hired man pulled back his foot to give Jack a mighty kick, but just before his boot met Jack's flank the smart old horse moved out of the way so that the man's foot hit thin air, making him lose his balance and fall on his back. Picking himself up, angrier than ever, he tried the kicking routine again, but with the same results. Reduced to pure exasperation, the hired hand turned the air blue with his cussing while Jack continued calmly, but stubbornly, to refuse to be hitched up. Finally Dad came to the rescue.

We had beautiful horses: King, Queen, Prince, and Flora, to name only four, and Carf and Art took almost as much pride in them as Dad did, combing and currying them until their coats and manes shone. In the wintertime some of the horses were let loose to fend for themselves on the prairie. They joined herds of other horses and roamed around in great bands, enjoying their freedom but sometimes turning up at the barn for feed. One night we awoke to the sound of our own horses' return and found they had brought with them many others, who tramped and snorted around in the yard. I was very young and frightened by all the whinnying and crashing of hooves through the icy snow. It turned out to be a sad occasion because when Dad went out to the barn next morning he found that a beautiful pure white horse had frozen to death after breaking its leg by catching it in a piece of farm equipment. I was haunted by that experience and many years later still dreamed of a huge white horse chasing me with its fiery eyes, blaming me for the great bleeding gash on its foreleg.

Carf and Art were responsible for milking the cows, and I loved nothing better on a winter's evening than to pull on my old clothes and tag along with them to the steamy barn, which smelled of sweet straw and pungent manure, to watch them strip the milk from the cows' bulging udders into galvanized pails that foamed to overflowing. There were always barn cats standing by, waiting for one of the boys to squirt a stream of warm milk into their open mouths right from the cow's teat. I helped fork clean straw into the stalls and carried oats and bran, which were stored in an old piano box, in a honey pail to the horses' mangers. I even helped the boys feed the squealing pigs, but one time they did a terrible thing. They threw my beloved teddy bear into the pigpen, and before they could retrieve it, it was demolished. It took a long time and a lot of coaxing for me to believe they were my friends again.

My brothers liked to hunt the big jack rabbits that roamed the prairies at that time. Some years the rabbit population was dense, and during the winter when the ground was covered with deep snow they came up to the buildings to feed, tearing the oat stacks apart and causing a good deal of damage.

Often, after dark, Carf and Art would take their 22 rifle and go out to see if they could shoot some of these night raiders. They were not hard to find; the boys had only to turn on their six-cell flashlight to see them jumping everywhere. On a moonlit night, the rabbits would be out in the hundreds, their collective paws sounding like the roll of distant thunder as they bounded across the snow. Unfortunately, the young hunters rarely had any luck with their night shooting, it being too difficult to get a good sight on the animals in the dark.

Carf and Art were each other's best friend. They rarely fought, but sometimes when they were wrestling around on the soft patch of chicken grass that grew outside the back door one of them would hit a little too hard and the friendly wrestling turned into serious battle. They pounded away at each other until Mother came running with the broom to knock them into their right senses, and they were soon pals again.

They didn't fight much with me either. Their teasing usually ended with an attempt to win me back into mutual good grace, and Carf could always make me laugh no matter how angry I was or how hard I tried to keep a straight face. He had the unusual talent of being able to wiggle his ears while sliding his scalp back and forth, and even though I might be very vexed with him, as soon as he started this silly antic I burst out laughing. Somehow, you can't stay angry when you're laughing.

When I began school, Carf was already attending high school classes in the upper room of the brick school while Art was finishing up public school in the village hall. They were very protective, and it was a boon to have two big brothers to fend for me. While they might enjoy teasing me themselves, they certainly weren't going to allow anyone else to pick on me. Because they were so popular, all their friends made a great fuss over me too. So, in a way, I was rather pampered.

The older I grew, the better I learned to take their teasing in my stride, and instead of being adversaries we became the best of friends. If I got into trouble at school, they never told on me; in turn, I never showed Mother the sexy magazines I found under their mattress when I was making their bed.

Both Carf and Art participated in sports, as did most of the young people of that time. Perhaps it was because there was so little money for any other kind of entertainment that sports were so important to us, putting challenge in our lives. In winter there were hard-fought hockey games and lively skating parties at Brock's small rink. Sometimes, after a Chinook had melted the snow into big ponds on the fields, a quick drop in the temperature turned the water into ice where we could skate. I recall one year we had a sheet of ice stretching for more than a mile, and what fun we had whizzing over the fields on our skates. That year, even Mother and Dad donned some old blades and wobbled around after us, laughing and falling down even when we tried to hold them up.

There were also sleigh rides down the coulee hills and, of course, curling. The boys laboriously hauled water from the well by the pailful to build a small, narrow rink in our back yard. This is where they taught me how to curl, our rocks being five-pound jam tins filled with water and frozen solid, with sticks stuck in the ice for handles. The boys practised in the frigid outdoors, and they could play better on the school teams that competed on sheets of natural ice at the rink. There they learned the game from A to Z: the strategy of skipping, the joy of winning, the sadness and inevitability of defeat.

In summer the whole community was fired up for the local baseball teams. Both Carf and Art grew up with baseball mitts in their hands, and their summers were consumed by the game. Art especially had a passion for practising for hours on end to improve his performance as a pitcher. As fate would have it, Dad hired a farm hand who had been a pitcher on several good teams in Saskatchewan just when Art was beginning to take baseball seriously. The man watched the young boy, who was small for his age, throw a few balls and decided there was enough talent there to make a pitcher. "To compensate for your small size," he told Art, "you'll have to concentrate on control." So control it was, and for hours every evening when the chores were done this hired man, Don MacLean, drilled Art on the out-curve, the in-curve, and the drop, with Carf taking the pitches in his

114

catcher's mitt. They both made the junior team without any trouble, but it was their dream to make it to the senior team. When they did, the whole family cheered. They were an awesome twosome, and how proud I was to sit with my friends and watch Art on the pitcher's mound and Carf behind the plate, both helping to win against teams that were much older and more experienced, and from far larger centres.

Often they didn't have proper equipment and went to Sports Days in other towns with no money in their pockets. Sometimes there was only enough gas in the old truck to get them to and from a game, and occasionally, when there was no gas at all, they took the wagon and horses. No obstacle was too great to dampen their enthusiasm or keep them from playing ball! Dad shared their fervor and, one time after an important game, he bought supper for the whole team. The boys knew, very well, that he couldn't afford it, but how happy and proud they were.

Later, when they both went off to Normal School, a year apart, I was left alone on the farm with my parents and George Shaver, our long-time hired man, who worked for little more than his keep and was like one of the family. Even though I spent hours with him, following him around as he did his chores, he didn't quite take the place of my brothers. I was often lonely for them, and I think they missed me a bit too, because they sometimes sent me funny notes imploring me to write.

When they got their first paying jobs, at tiny rural schools where salaries were minimal, they usually had a small gift — a fancy comb or a pair of bobby socks — tucked in their pockets for me when they came home for a weekend.

Our hired man, George Shaver, was like a member of the family. He married Ruth James, a daughter of my parents' friends.

Fortunately, they have remained my friends all my life, and I've never ceased to be thankful for such a pair of good brothers.

~

CHAPTER TWENTY-TWO

My Sister, My Best Friend

A s far as I'm concerned, having a big sister was one of the best things that ever happened to me, and I've always felt sorry for those who've never known the privilege.

Lola was born in Ontario in 1914, Mother and Dad having returned there for a spell after their initiation to Saskatchewan in 1913. Carf arrived exactly two years later on the same date, making him an extraordinarily special birthday present for two-year-old Lola. Art made it on the scene a year and a half later, and for the next six years Lola enjoyed her role as the only girl in the family. As the eldest, she also felt a deep responsibility for her two little brothers — while enjoying the authority to boss them around and play the games she chose.

As a toddler, Carf loved to sing, so Lola, pretending he was a gramophone, wound him up by his ear until he trilled his little heart out. When she tired of his music she simply pushed the off button, which happened to be his small snubbed nose. As they grew older and more daring the three of them loved to ride on the backs of the pigs in the barn, twisting their tails to make them run faster and hanging on for dear life.

One day when Lola was playing by herself, mixing up mudpies, an incident occurred that was almost the end of this special sister. Dad, who was hauling water to the cistern near the barn, left the planks that covered the top lying loose while he went off for another load at a nearby slough. Of course, that would be the very time when little Miss Lola decided to go to the cistern's pump for some water to stir up her pies. As she stepped on the planks, they slid out of place and she found herself falling into the deep cistern half full of water. By some miracle she caught herself by her elbows on the edge of the boards and hung there, crying for help. No one heard her, but she managed to work her feet up the side of the cistern and crawl out by herself. It was a close call, and a terrifying one, and when she ran to the house and sobbed out her story, Mother was so upset and frightened that she rushed out to meet Dad to scold him for his negligence. He too was shaken by this close brush with tragedy, and from that day on the greatest of care was taken to keep all holes and other dangerous places sealed up.

As I've mentioned earlier, Lola wasn't particularly happy when I came along, fearing her place would be usurped by this interloper, but she must have been won over very early, because I never remember a time when she wasn't kind, patient, and loving toward me.

She was more than a sister. She was my good friend and a second mother as well. Perhaps because Mother was so busy looking after the house and her farm chores, and because Lola was almost ten years my senior, much of the responsibility of bringing me up was left to her. It was she who taught me my prayers as we knelt together beside our bed, and it was she who taught me to count and know the alphabet long before I went to school.

She also broke me from a bad habit. I drank from a bottle and nipple until I was well past two, and when Mother finally did wean me I still insisted on going around with a dummy nipple in my mouth. No amount of coaxing or teasing could persuade me to give it up until one day when Lola and I were leaning out an upstairs window watching the big gray geese below. I hated those hissing bullies which terrorized me by chasing me around the yard, and on this particular day, as we watched them strutting and showing off below us, Lola purposely knocked the nipple out of my mouth so that it fell down among them. "Oh, look," she cried, "the geese have got your nipple!" That was enough for me. I wasn't going to tangle with those horrid creatures over any old dummy.

Lola told me endless fairytales as we snuggled under our covers and read to me the wonderful Honey Bunch books that May Clifford brought. They were about a little girl who lived in faraway England, a place with an enchanting sound that fed my imagination. These stories, and the ones Dad read to me, imbued a love for reading in me so that, later on, Mother complained about my always having my "head in a book," especially when it came time to do household chores! (I read all the books May Clifford sent out, many of them beyond my comprehension and some of them a little more risqué than Mother and Dad ever dreamed!)

To Lola I owe anything I know about housecleaning. Every Saturday it was her duty to clean the upstairs, the livingroom, and the diningroom, and from my earliest memory I followed her around with a dustcloth in my hand.

By the time she moved away, I was well-trained to take over her job, although I never became the thorough house-cleaner she was!

One thing Mother would not allow us girls to do was milk the cows. For reasons she never explained, she thought milking a cow was unlady-like, so no matter how pressed Dad and the boys might be, we girls were never allowed to help out, or even so much as place our hands on a cow's udder!

After her cleaning chores were done on a springtime Saturday, Lola often took me on walks across the prairie where we gathered the first delicate mauve crocuses while listening to the lilting song of the yellow-breasted meadowlark. In June we picked the wild pink roses that grew on the fence. Lola was my idol, and I ran along behind her, following her everywhere like a puppy until she teasingly nicknamed me Little Shadow. I must have been a nuisance at times, but I never remember her being out of sorts with me.

The small bedroom we shared had a slanted ceiling and was just large enough to hold a high bed, dresser, washstand, and an old trunk, which Mother had covered with pink and green cotton chintz that matched the curtains. Because of the slanted ceiling, the bed and dresser couldn't stand flat against the wall, and in the small space behind them, perhaps three by eight feet, I set up my winter playhouse with dolls, dishes, and orange crates. At the other side of the room there was a large walk-in closet where Lola and Mother kept their clothes, and I spent many a day dressing up in their

dresses, shoes, and hats, putting on concerts and sometimes even using the top of the dresser for a stage. If Lola happened in on me during one of these performances, she was much kinder than Carf or Art, never making fun of me, at least not to my face.

Later, when she was teaching, she had a beautiful pink and black satin evening gown and patent leather shoes with big shiny buckles. Sometimes, swathed in this elegant gown and clumping around in these shoes — far more beautiful than Cinderella's glass slippers — I attended pretend par-

Lola at 18, graduating from Normal School.

118

ties at the Queen's palace, bowing low to myself in the mirror. I had to keep a keen ear open for Mother, who would not have approved of my flouncing about in Lola's best party dress.

If I envied my sister anything it was her lovely looks. Both she and Art took after Mother's people, who were fine-featured, while Carf and I had the coarser features of Dad's side. Lola had dark bouncy hair, brown eyes, and dimples, and when I compared all that to my own mousy-coloured hair and skinny frame I felt like an ugly duckling. Nevertheless, when she was in her teens and getting ready for a date, I was happy to sit in the middle of the bed and intently watch her spit-curl her hair, carefully applying rouge, lipstick, and powder before adding the final touch, a black beauty spot on her rosy cheek!

When I was twelve, she took me to the beauty parlour for my first perm, and I was so excited I was sure my heart was thumping right through my thin dress. The discomfort counted for nothing as I sat still for what seemed hours having my short fine hair wound on steed rods and doused with an ammonia solution so powerful it made my eyes fill with tears and almost choked the breath right out of me. Then clamps attached to wires which hung from an electric contraption above my head were placed over the rods and the power turned on. In a few minutes I detected the smell of my singeing hair and prayed it wouldn't burn off at the roots. Finally, just when the heat became so intense I thought I'd have to call for help, the machine was turned off. The clamps and rods were removed to reveal a dry frizzy mass where my hair had once hung limp and straight. I though it was lovely, and primped in front of the mirror for hours after we got home.

Mother was determined that we would all be musicians, whether we had any talent or not! She played the piano a bit herself, and insisted very early on Lola becoming a pianist and Carf a violinist. Lola did become a credible piano player, and Carf, after torturing us with some dreadful scraping and scratching, did conquer the scales, and even played with some other boys at church and community functions. But his violin career was cut short when his teacher moved away. He turned to the banjo while Art took up the mandolin so that they, with Lola at the piano, made quite a lively trio.

Convinced that Art was going to be another Caruso, Mother made much fuss over his high tenor voice, dragging him in from the barn to sing for visitors, especially if she thought they knew something about music. No matter how he tried to hide or how loud his protestations, she insisted that his clear pitch would make us all famous one day. It might have, too, if he'd been more willing to practice, but he was only interested in pitching baseball, so Mother had to give up her dreams of his becoming an opera singer.

When I was old enough, even though money was almost non-existent by that time, Mother found the thirty-five cents a week for me to take piano lessons from Evelyn Groz, the daughter of the station agent. The Grozes lived in half of the railway station, and I loved going there, having to climb the set of steep stairs that reached their porch where Mrs. Groz always welcomed me with a smile and said good-bye to me with an encouraging word even though I might not have played very well. I never did become the pianist Lola was, however.

Lola and I became weekend sisters when I was six and she went off to Rosetown to finish her high school because the higher grades weren't taught at Brock. How sad I was to see her leaving every Sunday evening.

On Fridays I waited impatiently, sitting on the back steps until the car bringing her home drove into the lane. Skipping in circles and jumping up and down, I welcomed her joyfully, hanging on to her hand and her every word. And what stories she had to tell about going to school in the big town (of perhaps eight hundred people). Because she was pretty like Mother and gentle-natured like Dad, she was very popular and had many friends. She loved to dance and skate and had wonderful adventures to relate around the supper table Friday night.

One night her adventures were a little too exciting for Dad. She bragged how she and a group of her friends had taken up a dare and climbed through a small window at the back of the Rosetown rink to get in to see a hockey game without paying. To say the least, Dad was not amused, and laid down the law in no uncertain terms: she was never to take part in a prank like that again, nor, he implied with his looks, were the rest of us.

Sending Lola to high school in Rosetown for a year had cost Mother and Dad more than they could afford, but they were still determined that she would go on to Normal School. When she graduated a year later, it wasn't the end of the problems by any means. There were already 1,000 unemployed teachers in the province looking for work, and her chances of landing a school seemed slim. She begged to go to the North West Territories where she could get a contract to teach for three years at $5,000, an enormous amount in those days. Mother and Dad wouldn't hear of an eighteen-year-old embarking on such a venture, and Dad drove her all over the country so she could personally hand her applications to the trustees who were hiring for country schools. Luckily she did get a little school south of Eston, about thirty miles from home, at a salary of $500 a year.

In those days, many of the older students took the first two years of high school by correspondence with the help of the teacher who taught all the junior grades as well. Some of the boys in Lola's first school were only a year or two younger than she was and could have caused discipline problems had she not won them over by her prowess in sports, fanning the first three batters who came to the plate at the first recess! Still, they weren't above playing tricks on the green young teacher: putting dead mice in her overshoes and wiring her coat to a hanger. Once she sat down on some well-placed tacks, only to rise very swiftly, to the unadulterated glee of her pupils.

A few years later, she moved to another school where the pay was better but the students harder to manage. She had made a vow never to use the strap, but the big boys in this school were incorrigible, paying no attention and ignoring her attempts at discipline. Discouraged, she came home for a weekend to talk over the problem with Mother and Dad, who agreed she had to get it straightened out once and for all or resign. Monday morning they were as stubborn as ever, so she lined them all up, pulled out the strap, and went down the line, giving each open palm a mighty whack. Their pride may have been hurt more than their stinging hands, but from that day on she had no more disciplinary problems. Fifty years later, one of them admitted, "Lola was the best damned teacher I ever had!"

Two years after Lola started to teach, Carf left for Normal School, and Art followed in his footsteps the next year. By this time the Depression and drought were causing such devastation in the lives of everyone that it was impossible for our parents to send the boys to Saskatoon without Lola's help. From her slim salary she was able to assist with Carf's expenses, and then, when he got his first teaching job not far from her school, they pooled their resources so Art could go on to teacher's training too.

Teaching in those times was not easy. The little wind-beaten rural schools, their paint peeling, were set on the bald dry prairie with scarcely a shrub or tree growing near them. They were often isolated and lonely, and some teachers even lived in the basements or in an attached room called "the teacherage." Lola and my brothers boarded with local farmers but often had to walk two or three miles and were not only expected to teach all grades but to be caretaker and fire-stoker too. Keeping the trustees and the parents happy while playing an active role in other community affairs was quite a feat. It was a weighty job for youngsters just out of school themselves.

After Carf taught for a couple of years, he asked for a raise of $50 to bring his salary up to $450 a year. Although the trustees assured him he was worth the raise, there just was no way they could find the extra money. Thinking he had a good chance at another school, Carf regretfully decided to resign, but the trustees wouldn't accept his resignation, pleading with him to stay if they gave him a promissory note for the amount of the raise. He accepted, although he wasn't sure he would ever be able to cash the note.

Art's first job was at a tiny school in an especially poor area. He was still a boy himself, nervous, unsure, and not very happy at the prospect of facing a classroom. Besides, he had the misfortune of running into bedbugs at his first boarding house, which threw Mother into a panic, of course. On the weekend, he couldn't come into the house until she was sure he had been de-infested. Dad helped him take the problem to the school board, which found him another place to live.

When Lola and both brothers were all teaching, they usually came home for weekends, bringing other teacher friends with them. Many hours were spent around our diningroom table discussing all the problems with tyrannical trustees, petulant parents, and undisciplined children. One day while Mother was washing up the dishes and I was polishing the silverware, we listened to all this complaining going on in the next room. I turned to Mother and said, "I swear to you I will never, never, never become a teacher!" It's an oath I kept, but one I've sometimes wished I hadn't, because I might have enjoyed teaching after all!

No matter how old my brothers and I became, Lola continued to feel responsible for us and constantly worked out plans to our advantage. And although we always knew her advice was given out of her deep love for us and with only our good in mind, I must admit there were times when we resented what we sometimes called her "bossiness." Often her choices proved right, but we wanted to make our own decisions even if it meant making mistakes.

She could appraise a situation and make a quick decision while I always needed time to think things through. Things haven't changed. When visiting her recently we were about to retire when she asked, "What would you like, tea or milk?" Then, not able to wait for for reply, she pushed the milk toward me saying "Have milk, it's better for you." And that pretty well sums up Lola; she has your decision made for you before you can figure out what it is you want! But there's never been a malicious or mean bone in her body, and her gentle heart is filled to overflowing with love for family, friends, and many others she scarcely knows. If I were to make one criticism of her it would be that she has, perhaps, taken on the problems of too many people, giving of herself to the limit. Nevertheless, there's many a young person around the world who owes his or her chance at an education to Lola's generosity, and there's many a person in her own community who's been helped and encouraged by her deep compassion.

It's been a great honour to know her and to have her for a sister, and my life has been immeasurably better because of her.

~

CHAPTER
TWENTY-THREE

Hear the Pennies Dropping

"Hear the pennies dropping; Listen while they fall" we children sang lustily as our few coppers fell into the green felt-lined, wooden collection plate at the United Church Sunday School. "Every one for Jesus, He shall have them all." That pennies were important we all knew very well, but if perchance we had no money (as was often the case) we understood that money was not nearly as valuable as the love in our hearts. "If we have no money, we can give Him love; He will own our offering, smiling from above." Those words were very consoling to the poor children of the Depression.

We had little knowledge of religious doctrines; as was the rest of our lives, our religion was very simple. If you were good God loved you and you went to heaven; if you were bad you went to hell to live with the devil forever! Although there were no altar calls in our church and no "accepting Christ into your heart" or other outward religious "experiences," we certainly got the picture nonetheless, but in a quiet way. We were led by the words and actions our our parents and their friends who, for the most part, lived out their lives with faith and goodness.

Some of these people were our Sunday School teachers, George Krepps and Mrs. Helge Jacobson, to name only two, who gave unstintingly of their time and love to all the children, endeavouring to instill the values and ethics of Christianity. Before we were dismissed, the teachers sang this admonition: "Our Sunday School is over, and we are going home. Good-bye, good-bye, be always kind and true." And we sang back our promise, "Good-bye, good-bye, we will be kind and true." As they were kind and true themselves, we were led by their examples, even if we did not always follow them!

When I attended Sunday School in the Brock United Church, there must have been almost a hundred children who came from the surrounding countryside, so classes filled every nook and cranny. The one I remember best met in the choir loft with Mrs. Chant as our teacher. Her husband owned the hotel, and I always imagined it was a great cross for her to bear that he also ran the beverage room, since in my family drinking anything alcoholic was a terrible sin.

Probably Mr. Chant had to operate the beer parlour in order to make a living, because the hotel business had dwindled drastically. Of course there was the odd salesman who stayed overnight, some of the teachers rented rooms, and a few of the farmer-bachelors spent the winters there playing endless games of cards in the warm lobby while the cold winds blew across their frozen fields. But the hotel was a far cry from the busy hostel it had once been.

Whether or not Lucy Chant was embarrassed by the beer parlour and the fact that her husband rarely attended the church to which she was so committed, I really don't know, but I do know she was a beautiful auburn-haired woman and a talented artist dedicated to her Christian faith. She brought her deep sense of compassion to the little Brock community and also a lively interest in all the arts, which she shared with many others. Her sense of drama made Bible stories come alive at Sunday School, and with great enthusiasm we sang the songs she taught us.

The Sunday School picnic at White Lake (a swampy, shallow slough with a fringe of poplars growing around it) was the highlight of the summer. It was usually a hot day in July when every family in the church gathered to visit in the shade or take part in the games and races organized by the Sunday School teachers. We children loved nothing more than to watch our mothers see how far they could kick their shoes in the Kick Your Slipper contest because their aim was usually so bad that their shoes went flying in every direction, some of them even ending up behind them! Our fathers competed in the wheelbarrow race, and there were peanut scrambles, sack races, and three-legged races, all of which were hilarious when some of the competitors collapsed in great tangled heaps of bodies, legs, and arms. Then, after some of the little children had braved the grassy waters of the slough to squat down and splash water over their hot bodies, we were called for lunch, and we sat down to enjoy the mounds of sandwiches, cakes, and lemonade our mothers had prepared.

There was also Mission Band for us small children one Saturday every month, and Mrs. Chant again was the leader. She held us spellbound with stories from other lands, and in fact it was her enchanting tales of Japan that

124

made me vow that I would visit that country someday. Many years later, I kept that childish promise and found it just as charming as Mrs. Chant said it was, even though she had never seen it herself.

The little church that my Grandfather Abram helped build in 1913, and where my father was an elder.

Most of our neighbours attended the small white frame church on Brock's main street. In 1913, Grandfather Cann was one of those instrumental in having it erected, and helped dig out the basement with his horses dragging a big scoop. The congregation, originally Methodist, was joined by the Presbyterians during the first World War to form the Union Church until 1925, when it became part of the United Church of Canada.

The Anglicans met in various homes until 1928, when they built a lovely little church, and the Roman Catholics also met in homes until their church was erected some time later. But it was the little white church on main street that seemed to be the focal point of the community. Here everyone gathered for the annual Christmas concerts, the fall fowl suppers, and many other social events. A church wedding was certainly considered a social event, but unfortunately there weren't many of them because many young couples were too hard up to get married.

The first marriage I ever attended was not performed in church, but in the home of Mr. and Mrs. Bob Deakin. I'm not sure now who got married, but I think one of the participants had recently arrived from England. Since the Clendening and Cann families were invited, it was an exciting, happy occasion for Bubbles and me, who at six were agog at all the proceedings. It turned out not to be the bride, lovely as she was, who made the greatest impression on us, but a young woman guest from the city. After the ceremony, we were astounded when she nonchalantly lit up a cigarette and held it to her brilliant lips with a hand tipped with long nails painted a defiant red. This was a first for us on two counts: a woman smoking, and one having painted nails. While our mothers clucked in horror, Bubbles and I were deliciously delighted at someone daring to be so rebellious. We thought it would be fun to try those things ourselves, somewhere down the line!

A prairie wedding at Bob Deakin's around 1929. Bubbles and I peek out beside the young bridesmaid. We are wearing frilly organdy dresses made by our mothers. Our beloved Granny Deakin stands almost directly behind Bubbles. The guests included our parents, friends, and neighbours.

Another wedding that caused a stir in the community took place in the church. The bride and groom were not particularly well known to us, but we crowded in with all the others who didn't want to miss an event that would bring a little glamour into our rather quiet lives. As the groom and best man waited nervously at the front, the young bride drifted down the aisle, a vision of loveliness with her long golden hair shimmering in the sunlight and falling over the shoulders of her lace wedding dress. Her pretty red-haired bridesmaid in a flowing gown of yellow and green georgette ambulated close behind as the minister's wife played "Here Comes the Bride" on the old piano. It was the most romantic moment I had ever witnessed, but it was soon to be shattered. The minister had just begun to speak when the bride burst into tears. Shortly her tears were joined by those of the bridesmaid, until their sobs filled the whole church. Despite the discomfort and sideways glances of the onlookers, the wedding went on! Later, a rumour went around that the father of the bride had forced her into the marriage, but I'm not sure that was true. Perhaps it was just nervousness or, as my mother suggested, the "solemnity of the occasion." In any event, it ended up more like a funeral than a wedding.

The fowl suppers, held in the basement, not only raised money for the church but acted as an important social event in the community. It was a small band of women who laboured long and hard to prepare the home-grown chickens and turkeys, peel mountains of potatoes and other vegetables, chop cabbage salad, and bake dozens of buns and pies. Delicious smells wafted through the air as the tables running the length of the basement were loaded up with food which was heartily consumed by the congregation, friends, and neighbours amid much noisy good humour.

The older girls were elected to serve, moving the platters and bowls from place to place on the table to make sure everyone got his share. I was thrilled when I was thirteen or fourteen that Mother decided I was old enough to share in the honour of this responsibility. My horror when I dropped a gravy boat on the lap of an astounded George Krepps can scarcely be described. Both he and I were dumbfounded into silence as we viewed the greasy mess soaking through his best pair of trousers, and my embarrassment knew no bounds when one of the older girls marched up with a tea towel to mop him up and snapped, "Well, for goodness sakes, Gwyn, at least apologize!" I came to my senses, mumbled a few words, and flew outside trying to hold back the tears.

While the ladies cleaned up, the men ambled outside to stand around and visit and the little children played tag, running and shrieking round and round the church. Finally, the Reverend Mr. Miller called us into the church auditorium for the concert. Accompanied on the piano by Mrs. Bob Arnold, Louis Keil, the hardware merchant, always played the violin. He was an accomplished musician, but when we were little we were always afraid he might fall over when he closed his eyes and, consumed with emotion, bent and swayed over his violin. Mrs. Miller, the minister's wife, and Mrs. Pete Hettle sang "Whispering Hope" and there were also several elocutionists. I can still hear Dad reciting "The Wreck of the Julie Plante": "De win' she blow lak hurricane, Bimeby she blow some more ..."

At the end of the concert we all went home with our stomachs and our minds full, and the church had a few more precious dollars in its coffers.

As a little girl, church services were a time for dreaming. It was an evening service, the minister travelling during the day to outlying country schools to conduct church for those living nearby. In the dim light of the dark church I leaned against Dad, with Mother and Lola on my other side, and Carf and Art at the far end of the pew. Sometimes if I got bored I'd slide down beside my brothers, who weren't always the most reverent churchgoers. Carf, his face as straight as a poker, would sing words other than those in the hymnal so that while the rest of the congregation was rendering a solemn "Abide With Me," he might be mouthing softly, "Home, Home on the Range." It would send Art and me into a fit of uncontrolled giggling, causing Dad to cast disapproving looks our way while motioning me back to sit between him and Mother.

Shown on the left, I caused a fuss at Cradle Roll because Mother wanted me to stand beside Jimmy Allen (seated, far left). She had to pick me up and console me. Bubbles Clendening, with fly-away blonde hair, is seated at the far right, while her mother stands behind holding baby June. Laura Salkeld is right and centre (wearing long beads) with her hands on Bobby's head. Right of her is Verna Lamb with baby Bill. Next to Mother is Mrs. Allen, Mrs. Hyde, and Grandmother Cann. In front of her are my Cann cousins: Ted, Audrey, Enid, Gordon, and Jack (sitting on the ground).

Often, as the minister's voice droned on, I played with Dad's big turnip watch, swinging it on its heavy chain or listening to its hypnotic tick. Across the aisle sat the Allen family. Mr. Allen came from the same area in Ontario as my parents and owned the general store where we did all our shopping. The families were close friends, and the Allens had two daughters, Marjorie and Audrey, around Lola's age, and one son, Jimmy, my age.

From the time he and I were scarcely more than babies he'd peek shyly around his father, smile and wave at me, and I would smile and wave back. My brothers, inveterate tormentors, saw this as a wonderful opportunity to tease me about my "boyfriend." They kept it up until I began to ignore my little pal and refused to return his smile and wave. One afternoon when mothers and children met for Cradle Roll and to have a photgraph taken of the whole group, I was placed next to Jimmy. I burst into tears and the old picture shows me being held in my mother's arms, unhappy and teary eyed, while little Jimmy looks very perplexed. The sad thing was that I really loved him, and if it hadn't been for all that teasing, I'd have been happy to stand beside him.

When we were about five, word flashed over the telephone lines that

Jimmy had taken suddenly ill. Unbelievably, the next day he was dead. As far as I know, the doctor was never able to diagnose what struck him down, but since none of the other children in the area became sick, it must have been a freak virus. Jimmy's was the first human death I experienced. I had shed bitter tears when kittens and a dog died, but Jimmy's death was too incomprehensible to cry about. I begged Mother to allow me to go to his funeral; I thought it might help pay for the times I'd ignored his smile. But she wouldn't let me, saying I was too young. I'm sure I wasn't, and it might have helped to dispel the sadness and guilt that hung over me for days.

Shortly after, there was another death in the community. Mother and Dad got a late call that a neighbour who had been seriously ill, Jack Foreman, had taken a turn for the worse. They immediately set out for his place and stayed with his young wife and little girl until he passed away in the early hours of the morning. Later I overheard Mother telling someone that just before he died Jack raised himself in bed and sang in his weak but clear baritone voice, from beginning to end, "Shall We Gather at the River." That made a lasting impression on me, and I've never heard the hymn since without my mind going back to that sad time.

I awoke in the morning to hear my parents returning and bringing with them the distraught widow and her small child. The young woman's face wore a grief I had never seen before, and my small heart ached for the child, Evelyn, who no longer had a father. I couldn't imagine losing my own dear dad, and for days I was especially good and loving to him.

He did almost die when I was ten. I was enjoying my annual week of summer holidays with the Jicklings when word came that Dad was sick. I was concerned, but not overly so until another neighbour dropped in and I heard him tell the Jicklings, "I guess Alex Cann is in a very bad way." The stress of overwork and worry, the never-ending difficulty of making ends meet, had taken their toll. Dad had suffered a heart attack.

I was desperate to go home, but Mrs. Jickling persuaded me that it would be best if I remained a few days longer so Mother could give Dad all her attention. After three long days, the crisis passed, and Mother phoned to say it was time for me to come home.

She met me at the door, dark circles under her eyes from anxiety and lack of sleep, but she assured me Dad was going to get better, that he just needed lots of rest and quiet. I was allowed to tiptoe upstairs and slip into his room for a brief visit. The pale, haggard man I saw lying there had little resemblance to my robust father. My heart rose in my throat as I stood there not knowing what to say. Sensing my concern, he smiled and spoke softly, "It's all right, I'm going to be fine."

And he was, eventually, but it took long weeks in bed and several months of rest before he was back to hard farm work. In the interval, everyone pitched in. Carf and Art spent as much time as they could helping George Shaver, our hired man, and even I held the jute bags for him when he chopped the grain into feed for the animals. It was a job I detested, the chop dust flying up my nose, into my eyes and hair, and making my skin feel prickly and crawly. There were also, of course, all our good neighbours offering to help with the work until Dad was well.

While he was recuperating, I spent many hours at his bedside, reading to him or just talking about many subjects, including God. There was never any doubt in my mind where Dad stood with the Almighty, but I wasn't as sure about my mother. Sometimes when I peeked, I saw that her eyes were open during the prayer at church, and she never knelt beside the bed to say her nightly prayers as Dad did. Once, when I had the courage to ask why not, she replied, tartly, that it was quite possible to pray with one's eyes open and while lying down in bed. She had no use for people who "wore their religion on their sleeves while not practising it in their actions," and she often referred, rather disparagingly, to Grandfather Cann (rightly or wrongly) as being one of those!

One Sunday when Dad was still not allowed out of bed, Mrs. Strutt phoned Mother, who hadn't been off the place or had Dad out of her sight since he took sick, to ask if she'd like to attend the evening church service. She was hesitant, but Dad urged her to go, saying he'd be just fine. She wouldn't leave him alone, and since Lola and the boys were away, she told me I was being left in charge. I was petrified. "What if Dad gets sick again?" I demanded.

"He won't," she assured me. "And besides, I'll only be gone a little over an hour."

As the car pulled out of the lane, I had the sickening feeling that I wasn't up to the responsibility she'd left me with. Terrified that Dad might take another attack, I was sure I wouldn't know what to do, and that he'd die. Slowly I climbed the stairs to his room, laden with guilt that I felt so uneasy. But again it was Dad who soothed my apprehension by drawing me into a lively discussion about what I was learning at school so that we were both surprised how quickly the time had flown when Mother came running up the stairs looking refreshed and happier.

Dad firmly believed in keeping the Sabbath, and the thought of working in the fields on Sunday never entered his head. Of course the horses had to be fed and the cows milked, but all other work was left for the remaining six days of the week. But while Sunday School and church were a must for us children, he was quite lenient with the rest of the day, when we could read, listen to the radio, or visit with friends. One thing I was not allowed to do on Sunday was sing cowboy songs. I knew many off by heart, "When the Work's All Done This Fall," "The Wreck of the Old Ninety-Nine," and lots more. Dad always encouraged my singing but if on a Sunday I burst into one of those songs he always admonished me, "That's not a proper kind of song to sing on Sunday, Gwyneth." So I'd just hum it to myself.

Four years after Dad's own heart attack, there came a call on a December morning from a frantic Jessie Jickling. Her husband Will had just dropped dead. Mother and Dad left everything and hurried off to do what they could in such a sudden, tragic situation.

One thing that had to be done was drive the twenty-five miles to Kindersley to buy a coffin, so later that day Mrs. Jickling, Catherine, Will's brother John, and Dad started out. It was an unusually pleasant winter day, not very cold, and the roads were passable for the car. But as it did so often, the weather changed suddenly and began to blow up snow. After quickly selecting a coffin and tying it securely to the back of the car, they hastily started for home. The farther they went, the thicker the snow became and the wilder the wind blew, until they could travel no longer. Fortunately there was a farm house nearby where they took shelter for the night. Next morning it was still storming, but all the neighbours rallied around, bringing their teams, graders, and shovels to open the narrow road to the Jickling farm, and the sad little party finally made it back.

That was not the end of the difficulties, however. The nearest mortician was in Saskatoon, and it had been arranged by telephone to have him come out on the evening train and return to the city the following morning. Since the road had closed in again, there was nothing for Dad to do but drive a team of horses pulling a sleigh the eight miles to D'arcy to meet the nine o'clock train. Three hours later he was back with the undertaker, who commandeered Dad's help to prepare the body of his good friend Will in the kitchen by the light of the oil lamp. Then, after a scant two hours of sleep, it was time to hitch up the team and drive the man to the early morning train.

The storm had abated by the time of the funeral, and the small house was crowded almost to overflowing with friends who came from miles around to pay their respects to a good neighbour and offer their condolences to his widow and young daughter. It was the first funeral I had ever attended, and before everyone else arrived Catherine took me into the livingroom where her father lay. If it hadn't been that he was in a coffin, I would have thought he was asleep, and as I looked at his gentle face, which I had so often seen wreathed in a wry grin, I felt sad, but not inconsolable. While the minister conducted the service, I squeezed into a space on the steps leading up the narrow staircase, among people I had known all my life and from whom I felt such strength and comfort flowing.

I was fourteen, an age when one doesn't usually want to display too much emotion, but driving home later in the evening I leaned against my dad, and again, as I had when Jack Foreman died when I was very small, I thanked God my father was still with me. But my knowledge of life had deepened and I now realized that one could never be absolutely certain of anything.

The storm at the time of Will Jickling's death was only one of hundreds of blizzards we endured. Sometimes they were fierce beyond anything I can describe, with high winds and fine, thick snow which blocked out all visibility. When the Fahrenheit thermometer dipped to thirty or forty below zero, a storm could be very dangerous, and we often heard of people being caught out in one and having their fingers and toes frozen — and occasionally being found frozen to death. It's no wonder that Mother was always frantic if Dad or the boys happened to be caught in such a blizzard.

One thing you could usually count on if you were driving horses is that they would find their way home, seeming to have a sixth sense of direction. One day when I was out with Dad, it began to snow so heavily that we could hardly see and I began to worry about getting lost. "Don't worry," he told me, "the horses will take us home." And they did. Sometimes, however, the elements were too much even for them.

One winter afternoon, Dad was detained at a meeting in town and found it was already snowing and blowing hard when he set out for home in the dark. As the horses, facing into the blinding storm, tramped through the deep snow across the unfenced fields, Dad counted on them to find their way. Suddenly, he noticed that their tails were blowing the wrong way and they were no longer facing in the direction of our farm. Not understanding why they had become confused, he turned them into the wind again, but shortly after found they had turned around once more and were going with the wind. This happened several times until Dad was no longer sure how far he was from home. Eventually they struck a small ravine and Dad, recognizing the grade, realized where they were and headed the horses in the direction of home, making sure they kept facing the wind. But when they arrived at our gate, they made no offer to turn in, continuing straight on until Dad turned them back. When he got them into the barn he soon discovered why the horses had acted so strangely: an inch and a half of ice had formed over their eyes so that the poor beasts were completely blind.

Another time, when Carf and Art were about fourteen and twelve, they begged to go to a skating party in Brock. Dad refused their pleas because he was sure a storm was brewing in the dark clouds and the stiff wind coming out of the east. They kept pleading until Mother went over to their side, and Dad, with great misgivings, let them hitch the team to the old van.

Sure enough, as the evening deepened the winds picked up and it began to snow. By eight o'clock we were in the middle of a savage blizzard. Mother phoned friends in town to tell the boys not to try to make it home, but they had already left, starting out as soon as they had noticed the first snow. She and Dad hurried upstairs and put coal-oil lamps in all the south windows, hoping the boys would see their dim glimmer through the storm. A half hour went by and they still weren't home. Then an hour, and then an hour and a half. Mother paced the floor, scolding Dad for letting the boys start out, although she was the one who really persuaded him to give in.

Since they were trying to follow a trail over the fields, it was no use going out to look for them — another rig could pass right by without seeing them in that thick blizzard. Mother phoned town again in the hope that the boys might have turned back when they realized the fierceness of the storm. But no, they were still out in that freezing, blinding snow. That was one time when both Mother and I joined our prayers with Dad's.

Dad, keeping a vigilant eye from the kitchen window, yelled suddenly, "They're here!" and rushed out with the lantern to help the freezing boys into the house and get the horses into the barn. It had been a scary experience, and we all breathed prayers of relief and thanksgiving that night.

But if the blizzards were wild and frightening, there were other nights that were peaceful and gloriously beautiful, nights when the bright stars hung so low in a velvet, silent sky that it seemed God was very near. On one such occasion, Mother and Dad were again called to help a friend taken sick in the night, and they roused me to go with them. It was in March, just after a Chinook had blown in from the west, melting the snow and leaving the roads running with water. A grain wagon pulled by horses was our only possible way of navigation. As we bumped along the deeply rutted roads in the steel-wheeled wagon, the sky above us began to dance with northern lights. This was a phenomenon we often saw, but that night was one never to be forgotten as the sky blazed with shifting, vibrant colours which played across the whole dome of the hemisphere. I stood close to my parents, bound to them by the beauty of the night. We held our breaths and tilted our heads to the heavens where the lights arched and flowed in inexplicable glory. Mother squeezed my hand. "Surely God is with us," she murmured. "Surely He is!"

~

CHAPTER TWENTY-FOUR

Good-bye First Love

I n 1932, Dad's elder brother, Uncle Lawrence, his wife, Aunt Mary, and their six children packed up the agony of eking out a living from a drought-ridden Saskatchewan farm and moved back to Ontario. They had lived about a mile to the south of us on the land Grandfather Cann had taken up in 1912, but despite the proximity of our farms, I can never remember being in their house. It was one of the great sadnesses of my young years.

From the time he was a lad, Dad had admired and looked up to his brother, and actually it was Lawrence who first drew Dad's attention to Mother, pointing out to him that she was "a real looker!" And since the brothers were close, it must have been a great hardship for both of them that their wives didn't get along. To this day I don't know why they couldn't, but not only did they not speak to each other, they tried to ignore each other's existence, which was not always possible living in a small community.

I think whatever caused the rift between them happened because they were both young, both homesick (Aunt Mary was from Ontario too), both raising a family in the hardest of times, and both suffering from nerves that were often raw. Under those trying circumstances they perhaps said things that cut each other to the quick and couldn't be forgiven. It was not until they were well into their senior years that they finally had a reconciliation, which must have freed their spirits. I certainly know that it lifted their children's.

Many youngsters growing up in the West at that time had no relatives living close by, so it was especially sad that we, who did have cousins, were not allowed to mingle freely with them. However, despite our mother's differences, there was a deep bond beween us. We played together at school

Back to Ontario, 1932: Uncle Lawrence and his family leave Saskatchewan. From left: Gordon, Jack, Aunt Mary, Ted (in car), Mary, Enid, and Uncle Lawrence. Cousin Audrey missed being in the picture.

and Ted, a bit younger than Carf and Art, travelled around with them to ballgames while Gordon, the same age as I, was in the same class. The others, Enid, Audrey, Jack, and Betty, all had special places in our hearts too, and when they moved away there was a void in our lives.

Uncle Art, Dad's youngest brother, married beautiful Aunt Marion, who remains a favorite today at eighty-nine. While still a teenager, Art joined the army in the Great War, went overseas, and was gassed once and wounded twice, which caused him problems the rest of his life, including his blindness in later years.

He was full of fun, and we kids adored him and Aunt Marion. She had come to Saskatchewan with her widowed mother in 1909 and was one of the first pupils to enter the Brock Brick School in 1912.

Uncle Art courting Aunt Marion before he went overseas in World War I.

135

Aunt Marion's eyes were (and still are) as blue as any Saskatchewan sky, and her smile as wide as its horizons. Everyone loved her and wanted to be her friend, and many children, having no aunts of their own, lovingly called her Aunty Marion, something I always resented as a child, not wanting to share her with anyone else. But the love in her heart was (and still is) so great that she was impelled to share it with everyone, and not just with her nieces and nephews although, even now, I think we did have a special place.

For a while Uncle Art ran one of the grain elevators in Brock, and there were many days when I dashed out to catch the school van at the gate and purposely "forgot" my lunch pail so I could run into Aunt Marion's for lunch. Her lovely smile always welcomed me as she quickly set another place at the kitchen table so I could share whatever they were eating. It might not be much, maybe a fried egg on a piece of toast, but in Aunt Marion's shining, happy presence it was like eating ambrosia. She always whistled or sang as she bustled about, and although she suffered through some sad times, her unflagging spirit never gave way to depression.

Uncle Art and Aunt Marion had one son, Howard, a couple of years older than I. He was a stocky little fellow with big solemn brown eyes under a mop of dark hair. For some reason or other, when he started school the kids began calling him Chinky, and if they really wanted to torment him they'd run after him crying "Chinky, Chinky Chinaman." This made him furious and he'd fight back with fists flying. I didn't like it when they teased my cousin this way, but I had to admit that I thought the name Chinky suited him very well, and that's what I called him, too.

Aunt Marion, chubby little Howard, and their pet dog and cat, 1924.

One of the worst calamities happened when Howard had a horrendous accident at the rink. He was about twelve, and donned his skates to have some fun on the ice. While chasing one of his friends, the friend tripped and Howard crashed down behind him, the tip of the other boy's skate piercing through his eye. The days that followed were full of anguish at the possibility of his losing the sight in the other eye as well. It was a terrifying experience for a young boy, and later he endured the discomfort of being fitted with an artificial eye and the rude stares of many people. But with

136

Aunt Marion's love and unfailing optimism, he made it through, and adjusted well to his handicap. The sight in his good eye actually strengthened so that he has had excellent vision all his life and enjoyed a long, accident-free career as a driver of heavy trucks, a job that certainly required good vision and quick reflexes.

Howard moved to Ontario with his mother and father in 1937, which was only one of the twenty-seven moves Aunt Marion and Uncle Art made in their wedded life. Sometimes they only stayed a few months in one place before the urge to move came upon Uncle Art again. No matter where Aunt Marion was, however, her heart never left Saskatchewan and she remains a child of the prairie to this day. She is one of that rare breed who knows how to flow with the ebbs and tides of life, and although she has never been encumbered by, or wanted, much of this world's goods, she is the happiest, most contented person I have ever come across. She is still an inspiration to everyone who knows and loves her.

The year before Uncle Art and Aunt Marion left the West (1936), Lola, Carf, and Art, who were all teaching, managed to save enough from their meagre wages to take all of us on a motor trip to Ontario. It was an unbelievably wonderful event. Mother hadn't seen her family since the winter of 1924 when she and Dad had left the three oldest children with Grandma and Grandpa Cann in Brock and took me, a one-year-old, on the train to visit the Eastern relatives. There had been sadness since then; her mother, a sister, a brother, and a brother-in-law had died, but Mother was thrilled at the thought of seeing the rest of her family again.

As for me, having heard Mother weave so many wonderful tales about Ontario, which I imagined to be the most beautiful place in the world, I could hardly believe we were actually going there to visit all those aunts,

With "Colie" beside the 1928 Chev we drove to Ontario in 1936.

uncles, and cousins we'd heard so much about. I went around pinching myself, not sure it wasn't just another of my make-believe adventures.

Preparing for the 2,300-mile trip in our small 1928 Chevy and finding space for all our clothes, food, pillows, and blankets while still leaving enough room for the six of us was an exercise in excogitation for Dad. Since our box of a car had no trunk, he tied our suitcases on the top and on the running boards with pieces of stout rope and bindertwine, and we sat on the pillows and blankets while somehow finding room for the boxes of food at our feet.

Finally all was ready, and at six o'clock on a hot, dry July morning we started off on this elephantine expedition with Mother, Lola, and Art crowded in the back and Dad and Carf up front with me sausaged in between, the gear shift between my skinny knees. It was not the most comfortable trip in the world; many of the roads were unpaved and the narrow tires passed on every bump to those of us inside. We were lucky if we made 350 miles a day, and it took us a whole week to reach our destination. There were no freeways to lead us around cities in those days, so we had to brave it out and drive right through them, strange and teeming with traffic though they were.

Our most disturbing experience came while timidly searching our way through the busiest section of Chicago, which we imagined to be full of gangsters and a dangerous place to be! Our accelerator pedal stuck and the little car's engine began to roar unrelentingly. The ensuing hubbub stopped all pedestrians in their tracks as they stared incredulously at this strange apparition, this overflowing caravan with boxes and cases roped onto its sides and top and bearing a license plate from only God knew where. I squirmed down in the front seat trying to avoid their amused and condescending glances, but despite the embarrassment there was nothing to do but turn off the motor and sit there while the traffic built up in the lane behind us to the cacophonic blaring of horns. Luckily a policeman came along and soon stopped the cars so Dad and the boys could push us over to the side of the road. He directed us to the nearest service station and in an hour or so this band of rustic Canucks was wending its way out of that frantic city and breathing easier again.

If not a completely untroubled trip, it was still a wonderful one, as full of adventure and exciting sights as any Marco Polo journey. At night, for two or three dollars, we stopped at a small cabin along the side of the highway, where we cooked our evening meal on a beat-up stove and slept soundly on lumpy beds. Before turning in, we sauntered out to explore the territory, widening our view of the world in amazing ways.

138

Morning found us up early, Mother insisting we eat a hearty breakfast while Lola and I cut up sandwiches for our noon lunch. The farther we travelled east, the more prosperous and picturesque the country became. On our last evening we stopped at Battle Creek, Michigan, and rented a white frame cottage with green shutters and two huge maple trees hanging over its red roof. Nearby, a gurgling brook twinkled past, flashing with hundreds of fish. In all my thirteen years, I had never seen such an enchanting place. "If Ontario is better than this," I told my Mother, "it has to be heaven!"

Well, it wasn't heaven, but it did seem like it to us after having lived through years of drought in Saskatchewan, where shrubs and trees were stunted and the grass was brittle and brown. I could scarcely believe the size of the elm trees that towered like giant leafy umbrellas in all the fields, or the greenness and lushness of the lawns, or the brilliance of the flowers that lined every garden and yard.

Then there were all those aunts and uncles and hordes of cousins, all waiting to welcome us with open hearts, who fussed over us and treated us like rare and treasured specimens. For almost a month we travelled among them from home to home, soaking up their love and attention and consuming all the delicious food they placed before us so that every day was like Christmas.

It was a thrill to drive up the tree-lined lane of the original Cann farm between Arthur and Grand Valley where Dad's sister, Aunt Cora, and her husband, Uncle Charlie Densmore, lived with their large family. Here Dad and his own father had been raised, and as we picknicked on the sweeping lawn under black walnut trees a hundred years old with our Densmore relatives and our Cann cousins who had left Saskatchewan four years earlier, there was a great sense of family, past and present.

It was like a page out of a book to visit Aunt Mary, Mother's oldest sister, in Oshawa. She had married an English engineer, Alfred Hind, who had been with Scotland Yard before emigrating to Canada to become the Chief of Police in Oshawa. When World War I broke out, he immediately joined the army, becoming a major, and came home with an illustrious service record to take up the position of Oshawa's Chief Magistrate. Unfortunately, he died as a result of his war wounds after having served in this capacity for only eleven years.

He had been dead several years when we made our trip to Ontario, but Aunt Mary and her two sons, Lionel and George, still lived in the large gracious home Major Hind had bought many years before. To me it was like a palace, three storeys of white brick with cupolas, verandas, and fancy fretwork decorating the outside. Inside was even grander, large rooms with

A holiday in Ontario was a dream come true in 1936. From left, Art, me, Dad, Mother, Lola, and Carf.

oriental rugs, rich furniture, and gleaming silver. Uncle Alfred had travelled considerably, so the house seemed full of exotic artifacts. One of these treasures fascinated me. It stood in the spacious hall, which was lighted by beautiful stained glass windows, at the bottom of a wide, winding, dark oak stairway, and was a life-size pigmy carved in ebony and brought from Africa. As I stared into the immobile, dark face and ran my hands over the smooth black wood, I tried to get a sense of the strange, wild continent from whence it had come. The few days we spent in that beautiful house were like living in a lovely trance.

It was no dream, however, when I came down with my first bout of homesickness, of which I thought I would surely die. Mother and Dad, going off to visit friends in whom they thought I wasn't interested, persuaded me to remain with a cousin who had youngsters the same age as I. It was the first time I had ever been separated from all my family at once, and as I waved them down the unfamiliar farm lane standing beside my unfamiliar relatives, my heart sank within me. It must be difficult for someone who has never been homesick to understand just what a dreadful affliction it is. I was literally very ill, unable to swallow a mouthful of food or even sleep, with tears of grief were always welling up inside me. Nothing interested me, and although my concerned cousins tried everything they could think of to cheer me up, it was to no avail. In fact, it only made matters worse because it added a sense of guilt to my already tortured soul.

It was only three days, but I think I would have pined away had it lasted one day more. When our Chevy came tooting up the lane again, I was terribly ashamed of the way I broke down and cried, but I was never so happy in my life. Mother, who was well-acquainted with homesickness herself, was repentant at having left me to suffer this ordeal, so instead of receiving the severe lecture on not being a baby I had expected, I was showered with sympathy.

That was the only bad part of the whole holiday. The rest of it was sheer joy. We loved our relatives, and found that the lush fields of Ontario almost made us forget what the dry prairies were like. Everyone told us Ontarians were suffering from the Depression too, and I know many people were, but to my young eyes, which knew the hard times of the West, it didn't look that way. Lola and my brothers were astounded to learn that teachers' salaries were three times what they were getting in Saskatchewan and began to wonder if they were in the wrong province.

It was still good to get home again, to be with all our friends and familiar surroundings, and we all settled down to our routine — all except Lola. The idea of returning to Ontario had been firmly planted in her mind during our trip, and the next winter it sprouted and grew until, in the spring of 1937, she handed in her resignation and that summer left for Ontario.

This was the first break in our family, and a hard one it was, but though we were sad to see Lola boarding the train we held on to the hope that conditions would soon improve in Saskatchewan so she could return. That was not to be. After she wrote exams to obtain her teacher's certificate in Ontario, she not only got a good position in the town of Arthur but also met the man who would later become her husband. All this put an entirely different light on matters.

In every letter, she urged Mother and Dad to consider selling the farm and moving back to Ontario. They were hesitant; although times were still hard, the drought was beginning to abate, giving Dad hope that the end of the Depression was in sight and that the West would boom again. Even Mother, lonesome as she often was for her sisters, still wasn't prepared to leave the farm and give up all her good neighbours and close friends without a great deal of consideration.

The next summer, Lola, her fiancé Perce Jackson, and a cousin, Peggy

Hammond, motored to Saskatchewan, and Lola began immediately to pressure Mother and Dad to sell the farm. There would be more opportunity for the whole family in the East, she said; already she had Carf and Art considering the idea of going to Ontario to continue their education.

"There has to be an easier way for you to make a living," she told Mother and Dad as she looked around the rundown farm.

It was a most difficult decision for our parents, especially for Dad, who for almost a quarter of a century had poured so much of his vitality into the farm and into the still young community. The factor that made him finally decide to make the move was the thought of having the family separated. Lola, obviously, wasn't coming back to Saskatchewan, and at that particular time it did seem that there were better opportunities for Carf and Art in the East. After many sleepless nights, he and Mother agreed to Lola's suggestion. They would sell the farm and move to Ontario when the harvest was off.

Lola was ecstatic, and she then persuaded them to allow me to return to Ontario with her so I could start school in September. She said later it was her insurance policy against their changing their minds. It all happened so quickly I hardly knew what was going on, and it wasn't until just the morning before Lola, Perce, and Peggy were starting out on the return trip that Mother and Dad agreed that I should accompany them. What with the scurry of getting my clothes ready and packed, I had little time to understand I was about to leave everything and everyone I had ever known.

None of my friends had any idea. As it happened, there was a dance in D'arcy that night, and it was there that I made the startling announcement that they would see me no more. Bubbles was completely unbelieving. "You're just kidding," she scoffed. "You're not really going!"

"But I am."

I had recently acquired my first real boyfriend, Earl Smith, and we were as madly in love as any fifteen and sixteen-year-olds can be. If Bubbles was incredulous, Earl was dumbfounded. "I don't believe it," he kept repeating. "How can you do this to me?" After the dance he drove me home in an old Dodge coupe he had borrowed, and we sat in the lane until 4 a.m. discussing this stupendous, sudden turn of events. Stricken with the thought that we might never see each other again, we held hands and sang this sad love song over and over:

> We walked the lane together
> Laughed at the rain together
> Sang love's refrain together
> And we'd both pretend it would never end.

Then one day we cried together,
We said good-bye forever.
You're gone from me, but in my memory
We always will be together.

Like true lovers, we pledged it would be "our song" and that we would never forget each other. Then, after one last kiss, he was gone.

It so happened that Earl's path crossed mine again, sooner than expected, when he came to Ontario about four years later to train at a Royal Canadian Air Force station during the war. He spent many weekend passes at our place, as did several other boys from Brock, including Herb Strutt, Claude Clendening, Jim Ham, and Ed Cyr. Mother made our house a "home away from home" for them and many of their pals, so that weekends often found every bed and couch filled to overflowing. For a while, it looked as if the old spark between Earl and me might flicker into flame again, but it died down, and after the war we both married different sweethearts. Nevertheless, even after so many years, the old song, "Together," still warms the memories of my first love.

The morning after I said farewell to Earl, it was Mother and Dad I was hugging good-bye before I climbed into Perce's car heading for Ontario. I wondered apprehensively just what lay ahead.

~

Uncle Art and Aunt Marion

143

CHAPTER TWENTY-FIVE

Settling in Strange Places

I t was one thing to visit Ontario with my family as I had in 1936, and quite another to realize I was going to live there. Although I knew my parents and brothers were following in a few months, I also knew I could die with homesickness long before that. Luckily I spent the first weeks in Toronto with Peggy's parents, Uncle George and Aunt Maria Hammond. In their fun-filled home it was impossible to be lonesome.

They were a wonderful pair: Uncle George, Mother's oldest brother, a small wiry man who viewed the world through scrunched up, twinkling eyes, and Aunt Maria, short, plump, and white-haired, always full of bustle and soft laughter. They had a large family of grown children, some of whom still shared their narrow, three-storeyed house on a quiet street below St. Clair Avenue. Those who were married lived close by so that there was a constant stream of people going in and out.

The Toronto home of Uncle George Hammond and Aunt Maria, a most cheerful couple with whom I stayed when I first came to Ontario.

All of them were funny people, wise-

144

cracking and joking and tricking each other in a way I found hilarious. Having a new scapegoat in the house pleased them, and I was soon the butt of much playful teasing. Whenever I went out in the car with the fellows, Laurie, Elmer, Ted, or Lloyd, it was nothing for them to pull up beside the worst looking, most down and out bum on the street and call out "Hi, Uncle Alex, we didn't know you were in town." Or, "Sir, this young lady is looking for an escort, could you help her out?" As the poor bewildered man stared at us from bloodshot eyes we roared away, me blushing and collapsing with laughter.

Although they were the zaniest bunch I'd ever met in my life, I loved the way they took me, a green, unsophisticated youngster, under their wings and showed me the sights of the city. It was Laurie who furthered my education by introducing me to Sunnyside, a well-known amusement park with a Ferris wheel a mile high and so many rides and games of chance that my head spun. It was the wild terrorizing ride on the roller coaster, however, that almost undid me, leaving me so white and winded as I wobbled weakly off that Laurie thought I was going to faint at his feet. And I very nearly did!

When September rolled around I moved in with Aunt Rachel and Uncle Alfie Dales, who lived in the pretty village of Grand Valley, where I was to enrol in school. Mother and Dad had come from this area, and there were many other relatives to help dispatch the strangeness of moving to a new place. Grand Valley was (and still is) one of the loveliest small towns in Ontario, built on either side of the Grand River, its thickly treed streets lined with quaint buildings rising up placidly from the rushy green banks.

The Dales' household was also a most cheerful one, although not as raucous as the Hammond one in Toronto. It was presided over by Aunt Rachel, an older version of Mother, who often scolded Uncle Alfie, who in turn didn't pay much attention and who never got overly perturbed about anything. Meeting Uncle Alfie for the first time was very disconcerting because his eyes crossed so badly it was impossible to tell if he was looking at you or not. The strange thing was, though, that in no time you were so won over by his warm kindly manner that you didn't notice his eyes at all! Pat, their youngest son, was twenty-one, worked at the local creamery, and still lived at home. He was a handsome, popular fellow who introduced me to the rough, sometimes bloody, game of lacrosse, which he played with a vengeance. Off the lacrosse field, he was a gentle young man who bantered back and forth with me like an affectionate older brother, making me feel very much a part of the family. I was lucky indeed to have so many loving relatives on my side when I made the big transition from my home in Saskatchewan to my new surroundings in Ontario.

Besides boarding Pat, Aunt Rachel had two high school girls who lived at her house. Since there were only three bedrooms, one of them for my aunt and uncle and one occupied by Pat, I was put in with the girl boarders. They were sisters, timid and very quiet, but the amazing thing was that when Aunt Rachel announced to them that I would not only be sharing their room, but their bed as well, they seemed not to mind. They happily moved their things around so that for two and a half months we hung our clothes in the same tiny closet, shared the drawers in the one small dresser, and piled into the same bed every night. It speaks for the times, I think, that we had so few possessions we didn't need much space.

I dreaded my first day at the Grand Valley Continuation School, and my two quiet bedmates weren't much help, simply pointing out the principal's room and leaving me feeling more scared and alone than I could have dreamed possible. Shy, and feeling very unsure of myself, it took a long time to gather up enough courage to knock on the door and walk in with legs that felt like jelly. A tall thin man with receding hair glanced up inquiringly, but said nothing. With my mouth as dry as dust, I somehow whispered my business and handed him a letter from my Brock principal, Mr. Giselle. Running his eyes over it quickly, he tossed it aside and said, "I'm afraid since you're from Saskatchewan you won't be qualified to go into Grade 10, but will have to repeat Grade 9."

Disbelief and humiliation spread over me. Then I began to feel anger spurting up inside at this man's not so hidden insinuation that because I was from Saskatchewan my education wasn't up to par. Since Lola, who had taught in both systems, had assured me I would have no trouble, I drew myself up and informed the supercilious man (whose name I never bothered to remember) that I certainly could manage Ontario's Grade 10 if I was given the chance. Finally, in a most condescending manner, he agreed that I could *attempt* it, but said he would be watching, and if I took up too much of the teacher's time he would soon put me back to Grade 9.

It turned out to be nothing but a breeze! Since Saskatchewan had (and still has) only four years of high school compared to Ontario's five, many subjects, such as Latin, French, geometry, and trigonometry, were started in Grade 9, whereas in Ontario they weren't introduced until Grade 10. In those subjects I was simply repeating what I'd learned the year before and had no trouble at all, heading up the class in the first set of exams. Probably with a little work I could have tackled Grade 11, but I didn't want to press my luck with the principal. I had a hard time not smirking every time I met him in the hall.

It also delighted me to rub salt in his wounds by cleaning up the ribbons

146

at the school's field day in late September, dispelling forever, I hope, his impression that just because a kid came from hard-ridden Saskatchewan it didn't mean she had been deprived of a good education and a sound training in sports.

I must admit that the other teachers at Grand Valley were splendid, especially Mr. Henderson, who was the first teacher to indicate I might have a small gift for English composition and who planted the idea that a writing career might be possible. The rest of the people in that quiet little village were wonderful to me too, some of them old friends of my parents who loved to stop me on the street and remark, "My, you do look like your father, don't you?" My classmates accepted me almost immediately, and very soon I was invited to innumerable parties and going out on double and triple dates. We did crazy things like driving out to the country to steal apples from a farmer's orchard. I'm sure the farmer couldn't have cared less about the few apples we took, but we thought it was dangerous, high adventure. Although my stay in Grand Valley was short, it was a pleasant introduction to living in Ontario.

Out West, Mother and Dad took off the slim crop, sold the farm to Oscar Elviss, a friend's son, and all their equipment and most of the livestock and household goods at an auction sale. They left with $5,000, not much to show for all those hard years of labour. The church and community held an appreciation night for them before they pulled out, and although the good-byes of their many friends were sad, they were intertwined with good wishes for a happy and successful life in Ontario.

When they arrived in the middle of November, 1938, they came straight to Grand Valley before going to Dunnville where it was arranged they would live for a while on a small farm owned by Lola's Perce Jackson. I was so excited at the thought of seeing them again I couldn't concentrate in school that day, and when it was finally time for me to rush home from school they were waiting for me, their faces beaming with wide smiles. Hugging them tightly, I thought they were the most handsome couple I had ever seen.

I wasn't the only one who thought that. That evening when some of my friends called around, they peeked in the window to see what my parents looked like before they came in to meet them. "My gosh," whispered one, "your mother is pretty, and young too."

"Young," I scoffed, "she's not young, she's forty-eight!" Still, I was proud of their assessment.

After just getting nicely settled in Grand Valley, it was sad to leave, and I was even sorry to quit the school despite getting off to such a bad start with the principal. But of course I wanted to be with my parents.

Perce had bought a farm two miles out of Dunnville so he could have an airstrip and hangar for the Taylor Cub plane he flew all over the country to check out the several gas-drilling rigs he operated at that time. Amid some old swaying pine trees on the farm he had already built a stucco, two-storeyed square house with all the modern conveniences, and it was agreed we would live there while Dad worked the land and decided whether he wanted to farm or go into some other kind of business.

Although Dunnville High School was several times larger than the one I had just left, I felt a bit more confident when I walked up the wide steps and into the principal's office than I had the first day in Grand Valley. My reception was quite different too. Mr. Hellyer was the antithesis of the Grand Valley principal, and welcomed me with smiling round eyes set in a round, rosy face. His friendliness put me at ease at once, and when he escorted me, himself, to my new home room and introduced me to the teacher and students, he won my heart completely.

It's never easy moving to a new school where you are stared at and whispered about and treated like something from outer space, but there's usually at least one person who'll take pity on you and show you the ropes. In Dunnville, it was a dark-haired girl called Jean who guided me to the gymnasium when it came time for gym class and who helped me locate a locker to put my stuff in. She belonged to a rather cliquey group which met after school at a restaurant downtown to "blow the breeze," drink Coke, and smoke cigarettes. Very soon I was part of this group, but never completely at ease. One reason was that I knew my parents would disapprove of my smoking, and another was that these students looked down on farm kids.

In Saskatchewan, even in hard times, farming was a noble profession, and a farmer's daughter was as highly thought of as any. In Ontario at that time, and especially in Dunnville, which was an industrialized town and set in a rather poor agricultural area, a farmer was considered a yokel, needing pity and not quite smart. In fact, to disparage someone it was popular to use your most derisive tone and say, "Oh, he's just a farmer!"

Because I stayed in town to keep Perce's elderly mother company as often as I stayed at home, I was accepted as a town kid, even though I knew I wasn't. When I told Jean that my parents were farmers, she said, "I can't believe it. You don't look like a country kid!"

"How do country kids look?"

"Oh, you know. Hayseedy."

With Mother's talent at the sewing machine I knew I didn't look "hayseedy," and I knew many other farm people who didn't either. I must admit, however, that many Ontario farmers of that era *were* poor and rather badly

148

educated, hardly able to make a living from the depressed prices they received for their produce. Sometimes their children did look a bit shabby, adding to the stigma of being from the farm.

Jean's father was a salesman, but when she invited me to her home it didn't take long to see that things were anything but prosperous for her family. Later, when I asked her to spend a weekend at our farm, I'm sure she only accepted because she couldn't gracefully get out of it, and thought she was in for a real backwoods time. Her face spelled disbelief as she walked through our modern house, certainly not opulently, but tastefully decorated with Mother's artistic flair. "I though you said you lived in a *farm* house," she cried.

Gradually I made other friends, some of them from farms, but the best one was Laura, whose mother was cook-housekeeper for a wealthy family that lived in a big house even grander than my aunt's in Oshawa. Laura and her widowed mother had their own small apartment in the back of the house, but often when Laura invited me in on the way home from school we sat in the family's breakfast room sipping hot chocolate, or if everyone was away, we wandered through the large rooms, seeing how the other half lived.

I liked Dunnville, especially the school, where I think the teachers must have been among the best in the province. Never, before or after, did I have teachers who took such an interest in their students. Even after all this time I can still recall most of their names: Mr. Miller who made mathematics a delight, Miss Beard who could actually make you understand Latin, Miss O'Rourke who, despite her name, spoke French like a native, dear Miss Hartley who always ended her social studies class with a cheerful, "Health and weather permitting we shall continue this tomorrow!" There was genteel Miss Massey making history come alive, and crotchety old Mr. Dunlop who called us terrible names but who pounded a lot of science into our heads nonetheless.

Then there was my love-hate relationship with Mr. Campbell, the English teacher. One day he'd encourage me by saying that I might just have a chance of making it as a writer, *if* I kept my socks pulled up. The next, he'd tear to shreds a composition I'd handed in with a sarcastic, "Well, Miss Cann, if you can't turn in anything better than this, you'd better forget it." Years later, he told my sister I was one of his most promising students, but I wish he'd given me more encouragement and less discouragement. I suppose he thought I wouldn't keep "my socks pulled up" if he did.

Meanwhile, Lola and Perce were married; Carf was working in Cape Breton on one of Perce's drilling rigs until he could decide whether or not to go on to university; and Art was starting his apprenticeship at a pharmacy

149

in Toronto. Of us all, I think Mother and Dad were the least happy. We all missed Saskatchewan and our old friends, but we younger people were caught up in the excitement of our new lives while our parents were finding it much harder to resettle in Ontario than they had thought.

It's true, they were happy to be closer to their relations, but then they weren't seeing them every day, or every week, or even every month. And although some of their new neighbours were friendly enough, they found most of them aloof, keeping to themselves. They both missed the openness and frankness of their Western neighbours, and the close relationships they had had with them. Remembering them fondly, Mother often sighed, "I'll never have friends like that again." And, in truth, I don't think she ever did.

After the wide expanse of Saskatchewan, Dad found the small fields of Ontario restricting. With his trusty horses, he was used to working 640 acres of land; the farm he rented from Perce had only 75. The change was too great, and he knew he could never be happy farming in Ontario, so he began looking for a business to buy. Eventually he found a bankrupt feed and grist mill in Exeter, where we moved early in 1940.

At the same time, clouds of war were gathering over Europe, and fear pierced our hearts as we listened to that madman, Hitler, on the radio. As a small child I had heard such terrible stories about the First World War that the mere mention of it turned my stomach to stone. When we were holding our speaking contests at Brock, one of the older students, Esther Lamb, always spoke on "Why Another War?" and I would become so upset at the horrors she recounted that I would have to make up an excuse to leave the room. Although I was in more control of my emotions at sixteen, I was still greatly alarmed when I heard about Hitler and Mussolini marching into countries in Europe and Africa, and I prayed fervently that we wouldn't be plunged into war.

But we were. On September 3, 1939, two days after the Nazis marched into Poland, Great Britain declared war. Canada followed a week later. I remember the day clearly. We listened to Prime Minister MacKenzie King make the sombre announcement over our small kitchen radio on the Dunnville farm. Then I walked out into the yard. It was a beautiful fall day. A few puffy white clouds drifted languidly across an unblemished blue sky, and along the driveway Mother's low hedge of zinnias was ablaze with colour. It looked like a "God's on His throne" day when all was at peace. But we humans were at war. A shiver went through me as the winds whispered ominously through the dark, drooping pines, and I wondered if our lives would ever be the same again.

Of course, they weren't. The war brought an end to the ten-year-old

Depression; the days of unemployment and economic gloom were over. Most of the young men, and many women, flocked to join the armed forces, and the rest were quickly mobilized to take on the thousands of jobs that suddenly opened up in munitions plants. One era ended with the beginning of another.

As a school girl in Dunnville when I was sweet sixteen.

~

CHAPTER TWENTY-SIX

Journey of Love

The journeys of our lives start the day we're born and end the day we die, when we pass the road map on to those who follow us. The journey will take us many places and into many situations, and much of how well or how ill we fare along the way will depend on ourselves, on our choice of road and the decisions we make along the way.

There will, however, often be difficulties and dangerous hills to climb, roadblocks and detours we didn't set up ourselves and over which we seem to have little control. It's then that we have to dig deep within ourselves for the courage and faith to continue. The Great Depression was a devastating road-block to my parents and most of their contemporaries, one that wrecked their dreams and halted their progress. But they drew on strengths they hadn't known they possessed and came through it valiantly, finding courage in their simple but profound faith and support from their stalwart friends.

For their children, those of us who grew up during the Depression, no ten years affected us more. The marks of those days would be on us forever, not all good, but not all bad, either. In fact, some of our values are conflicting: faith tinged with a little *Myself and Art, 1933.*

distrust, courage with a sense of timidity, hope laced with some fear. But perhaps most of all we learned the strength that comes from love and the invincible consolidation that grows from sharing the good and bad times with those closest to you.

Born Again Bath _____

How I love baths!
This evening as I soak in bubbled water,
Lathering heavy-scented birthday soap,
My childhood baths return to me ...
Taken before a roaring fire in our kitchen,
More luxurious than the one I'm having now,
For heat was not a thing we took for granted
In that slack house where lawless western winds
Invaded every crook and crack.

Hot water was doled out with care
From the crackling range's reservoir
Or heated on the top in pails.
Most of our neighbours bathed
In round washtubs of tin,
But we had a magnificent affair,
Something like a camp cot of gray rubber,
Unfolding to a full-size tub
You could stretch out in,
Breathing in the steamy lye from
Homemade chunks of creamy soap.
And, oh! the scrumptious pleasure of
Drying on striped towels warmed on the oven door;
Pulling on a toasted flannel gown
And then, heels flying,
Down the dark and icy hall
To beds of eiderdown,
heated by two hot bricks
Wrapped in newspapers.
I swear it was like being
Born Again!

We had a ritual at our house ...
Because I was the smallest
And used the "leastest" water,
I was the first to bathe.

153

More hot was added for my sister,
And still another pailful for my mother.
I envied my big brothers
Who bathed together
With water almost to their necks!

Finally, it was my father who embarked
Upon this weekly cruise of cleansing.
Mother, laughing softly, scrubbed his back,
While flickering yellow flames
Cast dark, mysterious shadows
On patched linoleum ...
Anthony and Cleopatra
In a snowbanked
Prairie home.

Thank God for baths,
   for memories,
   for love,
   for care,
   for sharing. _____

~

EPILOGUE

oon after my parents and I settled in Exeter, Carf and Art joined Dad in operating the grain and feed business. Over the years it grew to be one of the most successful in the area.

The years in Exeter were happy and peaceful for Mother and Dad. They enjoyed having their children and grandchildren close by and they made many good friends in the town. No one ever took the place of the Saskatchewan friends, however, and they were never happier than when they were planning a trip out West to visit them.

They continued deeply committed to each other, Mother jealous if another woman so much as glanced at Dad. When I was twenty I broke my engagement to a young man of whom she was extremely fond. When she demanded a reason for my drastic, and to her mind foolish, action, I replied wryly, "I just couldn't bear the thought of sitting across the table from him every day for the next fifty years of my life."

"Fifty years!" she exlaimed passionately. "Why, fifty years isn't half long enough for me to sit across the table from your dad!"

Then she smiled, "I guess you really *don't* love the boy."

Mother remained feisty and creative almost to her dying day. When she passed away in 1972 at the age of eighty-one, she left behind a large inheritance of beautiful things she had made and collected. Up to her final illness, Dad continued to care for her, looking after her every need until she was admitted to hospital about a week before she died. They had just celebrated their sixtieth wedding anniversary.

Four years later, a prostate gland operation revealed that Dad had cancer. It appeared that the operation had arrested it, but a few months later, when

155

he and I stood in the cancer specialist's office to view his latest x-rays, it was evident to even our laymen's eyes that the disease was spreading rapidly.

It was a blow to both of us, but after we arrived back at his apartment it was he who comforted me. "It's all right, you know. I always said if I lived to be eighty-five I'd be content to die."

But I was not content to let him go. Neither were Lola, Carf, and Art. At eighty-five, he was still vigorous and alert. It was hard to accept that his life was coming to an end.

After the diagnosis, he went to hospital for special treatments. He was in an area where all were elderly and chronically ill. The room was small and the old man next to him, tied to his bed and his mind almost gone, rattled the bed rails constantly. In despair I watched my father quietly retreat into a shell, his eyes losing their sparkle. There had been talk of a series of cobalt treatments, but after further examination, the doctor shook his head. They would serve no purpose and only add to Dad's discomfort.

I was surprised that I met this news with profound relief. I prayed, "Take him if you must, dear God, but please, no more hospital." And so Dad went home to stay.

He functioned normally and happily. Except for some pain, a growing tiredness, and a slow loss of weight, he carried on his routine, cleaning his apartment, cooking his meals, and visiting friends. Since I lived on the same block and Carf was close by, we checked on him a couple of times each day.

On Father's Day we had a grand celebration. His four children, his grandchildren, and his great-grandchildren gathered to shower him with love and esteem. He beamed with pride as he surveyed us all in response to a toast given by his grandson Roger, Art's son. It was a perfect day overflowing with happiness and thanksgiving.

As it turned out, it was Dad's going away party. Almost immediately he began to slip. Within two weeks we could scarcely believe the change. Lola, now a widow and living 130 miles away, moved into his apartment. With Carf's and my help, she took care of him for two or three weeks. Art, who lived in another town, came as often as he could.

Each day found Dad weaker and stiffer. Only with the greatest of difficulty could we move him from bed to his favorite chair.

"What are you going to do with me?" he asked one morning. "Perhaps we could find a nursing home."

"And what's wrong with this home," I teased him. "Not satisfied with the help?"

"But it's too much for you!"

"When it's too much for us, Dad, we'll let you know."

156

Lola began to stay only at night while Carf and I took on the day shifts. Later, I started to keep the watch every second night so Lola could go to my home to sleep. Rest was virtually impossible for both Dad and whoever stayed nights.

I was hesitant to tell the doctor we were hoping to keep Dad at home, but it turned out he was sympathetic. "Good," he replied, "Keep him here as long as you can, right up to the end if possible. It will be better for him, and for you too."

We enlisted the help of the Victorian Order of Nurses and Home Care. The nurses were kind and considerate, handling Dad gently and advising us in so many ways how we could better care for him ourselves.

During the last three weeks, Lola, Carf, and I took the day shifts until midnight when the Home Care helper came on duty. For the last five nights, when it seemed Dad might slip away at any time, we hired a registered nurse, kind and experienced with the dying, to stay with him.

The night before he passed away, he slipped into a deep sleep from which he never awakened. The body, however, did not give up easily. It fought to contain the spirit, the breathing heavy and laboured as the struggle went on.

Carf and I were alone with him at mid-afternoon, wiping perspiration from his dear face now filled with dark hollows, dribbling water into his open mouth, praying his ordeal would soon be over. Suddenly, his breathing and colour changed. Carf took his pulse. "It's going."

While I cradled his head in my hands and Carf held his body, the tired old heart finally ground to a stop and the precious face relaxed. "Thank God," we breathed, but our meeting eyes burned and brimmed over.

The struggle was finished. No more the painful turning in bed, or the effort to swallow the pills or a few spoonfuls of food, or the agony of aching muscles and bones. He had been so patient through it all, never complaining, always trying to make it easier for us, as he had done all his life.

In the final weeks, his voice had almost left him. Yet he would express his love in so many ways. Once when I bent to kiss him goodnight, his eyes filled with tears. "Ever since you were a little girl ..." his whisper trailed off, but I knew he was saying he loved me.

Another time, he beckoned for Carf to come closer, then lifted tired arms to enfold him in a weak hug. To Art and Lola, too, he expressed how much he loved them with every look.

And so, after a full and gracious life, he left with no regrets. For him, it was a welcome release to the new life he was certain would be his. For us, it had been a joyful task to ease his passing from this world to the next.

157

As we watched the gray hearse pull away, Carf summed it up for us. "It's been the greatest privilege of my life to help care for Dad during his final days on this earth." Yes, the burden had been light, just a small parting gift to a wonderful father.

Mother and Dad in Exeter.

~